The Beginning of the Gospel

Mark's Story of Jesus

William Peatman

A Liturgical Press Book

THE LITURGICAL PRESS
Collegeville, Minnesota

BS
2585.2
.P43
1992

Cover design by Greg Becker

Quotations from the Gospel According to Mark are from the Revised Standard Version, Catholic Edition, 1965.

Copyright © 1992 by The Order of St. Benedict, Inc., Collegeville, Minnesota. All rights reserved. No part of this book may be reproduced in any form or by any means, electronic or mechanical, including photocopying, recording, taping, or any retrieval system, without the written permission of The Liturgical Press, Collegeville, Minnesota 56321. Printed in the United States of America.

1   2   3   4   5   6   7   8   9

Library of Congress Cataloging-in-Publication Data
Peatman, William.
    The beginning of the Gospel : Mark's story of Jesus / William Peatman.
      p. cm.
   ISBN 0-8146-2068-X
    1. Bible. N.T. Mark—Criticism, interpretation, etc. I. Title.
BS2585.2.P43 1992
226.3'06—dc20   92-18813
                                                     CIP

For Christa

Contents

Acknowledgments 6

Introduction 7

1 The Beginning of the Gospel: Repentance 13

2 The Beginning of the Gospel: Rescue 19

3 The Beginning of the Gospel: Faith 25

4 The Beginning of the Gospel: Love 31

5 The Beginning of the Gospel: Friendship 37

6 The Beginning of the Gospel: Honesty 47

7 Conclusion 57

Acknowledgments

I would be remiss if I did not acknowledge the influence that a small group of Christians at Yale University have made on my life and my faith. As a campus minister there from 1985–1990, I was called to serve them but, as is so often the case, I received much more than I gave. Keith Cooper, Tom Musbach, Todd Hartch, Jennifer Oyama, Kathy Schaal, Melissa Waters, and Scott Beers, among others, gave me a great deal of insight and inspiration in the struggle to follow Jesus. I believe that what we experienced was, at its best, the beginning of the Gospel. I would also like to thank Jeff and Leslie Woodward who helped me to write this book in so many ways, and who at various points in my life have carried me.

Introduction

Discovering God is really like coming home. G. K. Chesterton once said that the story he'd most like to write is about a man who leaves England to explore new worlds, only he gets lost and ends up returning to England, and explores it like it is a new world. He would find, Chesterton insists, that the adventure, delight, terror, and mystery that he was looking for had been surrounding him all along.

That is the same experience that a young boy has in Jesus' story we've come to call the Prodigal Son (Luke 15). We're told that a boy asked for his inheritance before his father had died, and when he got it he left home in search of a life of greater adventure and satisfaction. He wants to indulge himself, fill his senses. Like most of us, he wants it all, now—all the happiness he can possibly experience. But it all comes apart for him in the end, and in the end he returns home, empty and ashamed, and resigned to a life of dullness and frustration.

But when this boy returns to his father, expecting anger and punishment, he instead finds, to his surprise, everything that he had been searching for when he left home. The father rushes to meet his son and lavishes his love upon him, breathlessly saying "I'm glad you're back." He gives the boy the best of everything—a fine robe, a ring of authority, and kills the fatted calf saying, "We must make merry, have a great party, and celebrate, for my son was dead, and now he lives." And he invites the whole town to a party with the son as the guest of honor.

The boy comes home to find that his father is not a boring taskmaster but a host of a brilliant banquet. He comes home to find home is a place that is brimming with love and joy, and that the father longs to satisfy all of the boy's desires. The boy rediscovers his home, his family, and he finds it stranger, more wonderful, and less predictable than he had thought; and my guess is that he knows he could explore that place, searching out and discovering his father's true nature, for the rest of his days.

All of us must leave home in order to rediscover its wonder and its charm. There is mercy there, and acceptance, that can touch us and fill us in a way that is hard to find elsewhere. For some of us home is a place mainly of pain. Some of us come from what have been called broken homes. They are broken not because parents have separated but because the hearts of each member of the family have been fractured. For some the analogy of coming to God as coming home is more powerful, for it means returning to find what home should have been like. Home is meant to be a place where we find love, acceptance, and affirmation. We come to God and something inside us shouts "yes, this is what home should be." Home should be a place governed not with force but where the law of the house is mercy.

Spiritually, the biblical writers teach us, we all do leave home. We all have turned away from God at one point, assuming that what we really desire can only be found somewhere else, but surely not from the hand of that old stick-in-the-mud. My hope in writing about Jesus is to return home for a visit, to approach it with the eyes of an explorer, and to come to the gospel as we would come to a foreign land. It may not be foreign to you, but if you can imagine that you have never been here before, you may discover something wonderful, or rather someone wonderful. This world, with God at its center, has been there all along, and in a way we have all been living in it. Then, in an instant, the lights go on and we find that all we really want has been surrounding us all the time, and that Jesus, the end of all our hearts' desires, has been only a heart-beat away.

This brings to mind the truth that, in a way, our true home is somewhere else, and if we are wise we will spend this life making our way back. None of us feel completely comfortable, or at peace, in this world. Our real home is with God, and the Bible provides us with a rough, adventurous map of how to get back.

It isn't a precise map like the ones we use to drive cross-country, drawn to scale, with exit numbers and mileage measurements. It's more like a pirate's map that will lead to buried treasure, full of mysterious places and coded terms. We are not told to take Exit 35 onto Highway 99, but we're told to look for a shepherd and be prepared to go with him through the Valley of the Shadow of Death. We're told to carry a cross somewhere, we're taught how to win thrilling battles with the weapons of love and humility. Most importantly, though, we're told of a treasure so breathtakingly rich and beautiful that if we were to look straight at it we would die of awe. This map speaks of places, experiences, and people, and they all conspire to lead us to God. And in the end this map, though mysterious at times, is terribly dependable.

The Bible means different things to different people. For some, the Bible represents harassment. Some of us have heard angry quotations from parents, spouses, children, in-laws, or from someone else who intends to correct what they consider poor behavior. For others the Bible is a burden—a legal code they feel obligated to attempt to keep, and keep it they do, for the pain of guilt if they don't is often more frightening than the labor of joyless obedience. And for others the Bible, selectively read, is pure encouragement—unbridled affirmation of their value as children of heaven.

For most of us the Bible is all of these things at one time or another, until finally it becomes what it is meant to be—a map that leads to a spectacular treasure. It begins with human words, spoken originally in Hebrew or Aramaic or Greek, and then translated into English by ordinary men and women with jobs, families, and mortgages, struggling and sometimes failing at work and at home. This book comes to us through the centuries, through the errors and corrections in text, and through the theologies and idiosyncrasies of its translators and commentators. And, remarkably, these human words sometimes—though not often enough—seep inside us. Words of Moses, of Isaiah, and most of all words of Jesus slip into the interiors of our lives, usually when no one is looking. These ordinary words are not ordinary at all, for they sneak in and pick the locks on our hearts, releasing a tide of pain that has gathered over the years and replacing it with the shattering love of God.

When I first read the New Testament after my freshman year of college, I made sure I did it when no one was looking. It was embarrassing to read the Bible and certainly anachronistic, I thought. So I read it at night, by flashlight, so that when my roommate would come in I could shove everything under the covers and pretend to be asleep. Not a heroic way to come to faith, but a good enough way for me at the time. I can remember the first time the flashlight's beam spread across these words: "What does it profit a person to gain the whole world and forfeit their life? For what can anyone give in return for their life? (Mk 8:37, 38). What I heard when I read those words was not a reprimand, but Jesus saying "Don't short-change yourself! If you owned the whole world, and missed knowing me, it would be a terrible loss."

My world began to fall apart and come back together with those two sentences. I knew I would never come close to gaining the whole world. I was driving myself crazy just to hang onto a small, small piece of it. Studying, wanting to make my parents proud of me, trying to make friends and be acceptable to my peers, worrying about the future. What was it profiting me? Very little. What would it profit me if I got all that I was looking for? Probably more of the same. More people to please and impress. More pressure to continue to succeed. Perhaps a few benefits I could really enjoy—money, possessions, reputation. But for some reason, lying in bed, the flashlight stopped on those words and for the first time in my life I was able to admit that I was unhappy and afraid. For the first time Jesus Christ was attractive to me. If he had this "life" that was better than the whole world, and if he was willing to share it, I felt that following him might be worth a try.

I went on to read the rest of the New Testament that summer. It became a series of shocks and surprises—especially in the Gospels. By the end I knew I was like the man in Chesterton's imagined story. I had gone to church often in my life, but the world of God had never seemed attractive or worth exploring. Then, finally, I chose to explore the New Testament only to realize I had stumbled upon Jesus. As I poked around to see what I had found, I discovered him to be more like a treasure than I had ever imagined. I found that Jesus was a source of more beauty, joy, and pleasure than I thought was possible to experience. And so I began the exhilarating process of selling all I had in order to know him and follow him.

I want to write about a small part of Jesus's life, and I hope to communicate a fraction of who Jesus is and what he is really like, and how the Bible is a book of brilliant, life-changing things. I've included some of the text of the Gospel according to Mark, and have drawn some observations from that. Scholars tell us Mark was one of the first people to write down what the first followers of Jesus experienced—the treasure that they found when they found him. My hope for myself and for anyone who reads this is that they will find the same treasure, and do whatever it means for them to enjoy it and hang onto it.

Try and imagine what it would be like to be one of the first people to come into contact with Jesus. You are there, and he comes by. That is what the Gospel of Mark is an attempt to do. After a few introductory remarks Jesus appears and starts his ministry. We are there. We respond not to a Church, not to a legal code, not to a political agenda, but to a person. This is not about religion, not even about Christianity. It's about Jesus.

A group of men and women met someone whose love for them was so shocking, so alarming, that they struggled for years to put this experience into words. The Gospel of Mark is one group of people's attempt to express their experience of Jesus. The book has been ever since, for millions of people, the beginning to the gospel.

CHAPTER 1

The Beginning of the Gospel: Repentance

> The beginning of the gospel of Jesus Christ, the Son of God. As it is written in Isaiah the prophet, "Behold I send my messenger before thy face, who shall prepare thy way; the voice of one crying in the wilderness: Prepare the way of the Lord, make his paths straight"—John the Baptizer appeared in the wilderness, preaching a baptism of repentance for the forgiveness of sins. And there went out to him all the country of Judea, and all the people of Jerusalem; and they were baptized by him in the river Jordan, confessing their sins. Now John was clothed with camel's hair, and had a leather girdle around his waist, and ate locusts and wild honey. And he preached, saying "After me comes he who is mightier than I, the thong of whose sandal I am not worthy to stoop down and untie. I have baptized you with water, he will baptize you with the Holy Spirit."
>
> In those days Jesus came from Nazareth of Galilee and was baptized by John in the Jordan. And when he came up out of the water, immediately he saw heaven open and the spirit descending upon him like a dove; and a voice came from heaven, "Thou art my beloved Son, with thee I am well pleased."
>
> The Spirit immediately drove him out into the wilderness. And he was in the wilderness forty days, tempted by Satan; and he was with the wild beasts; and the angels ministered to him.
>
> Now after John was arrested, Jesus came into Galilee, preaching the gospel of God, and saying, "The time is fulfilled, and the kingdom of God is at hand, repent, and believe in the gospel."

Jesus steps straight from eternity onto the first page of the Gospel of Mark. No Christmas story. No genealogies. Just a few words of Old Testament prophecy, their fulfillment first in John the Baptist, and then in Jesus himself. John the Baptist, that dazed and delirious preacher who knew something was going on before the rest of the world. He knew who was coming and he was crazy with joy. He knew the one was coming who would wipe away every tear, the one who would catch our cries of pain before they escaped our hearts and replace them with the Spirit of God. John was crazy with a joy that made him brave—telling everyone, no matter what position they held in the world, that it was time to take a look at your life, and admit that it wasn't as good as you wanted it to be. He knew like no one else that his life, and indeed the whole planet, was in God's hands more than ever at that particular moment.

After a few sentences we're told, "Now after John was arrested Jesus came into Galilee, preaching the gospel of God, saying 'Time is fulfilled, the kingdom of God is at hand, repent and believe in the gospel.'"

Everything else fades into the background like the opening scene of a play when we find out who is the star of the show. Jesus takes center stage. He emerges from the scene full of characters and information—Isaiah's prediction, John's preparation, baptism, temptation. Then the others all fall away because they are there to call attention to the star, and so Jesus stands alone and begins his song.

Time is fulfilled. Time has finished spinning its web of lines and circles. Every human life is one of those threads that moves time forward. History is coming to its conclusion in some unimaginable way.

The kingdom of God is at hand. The world of God, ruled and tended by him, is suddenly at hand and within your reach. It is available and it is so close you can touch it.

Repent and believe in the good news. Repent! Turn around! Finally some news worthy of your attention; some news that is truly good. Something so wonderful it causes you to snap your head around to listen.

Repent must be the most unpopular word in the English language. It's not a bad word. It's not meant to condemn, though have on other people. She summed it up this way: "The one thing I'm certain about is that now I love God."

God reached out to her, and she took his hand the first time she saw it. I did not take his hand at the time of my first sighting. Perhaps I shouldn't have. Perhaps I wasn't ready. Or perhaps I missed a dozen more years of living in a world of brilliance, a world of wonder. I don't know, and it probably doesn't pay too much to speculate on the past. The issue of course is the present, and letting him lift us today into repentance and belief and a new life in the world where God is king, the kind of king who takes each subject, personally, by the hand.

real and he loved me. I knew it for certain. I knew it perhaps with a kind of certainty that I have not known since.

Was that Jesus offering his hand? Was that Jesus, shouting in the stillness and beauty of a Christmas moment "turn around!"? Was that him, shouting in a way that was so quiet and reassuring that it could make the word "repent" feel like an embrace?

It was a flash. Jesus flashes into our lives and our hearts at certain times, in a fraction of a second. Paul tells us that in the last moment of time Jesus will appear as quickly as a wink of an eye. He comes quickly, unexpectedly, sometimes even uninvited. And we really do see him. Perhaps at Christmas. Perhaps through an act of kindness toward you that convinced you that you were loved in a way that was deeper than any human could have spoken to you. Or perhaps it was in an act of kindness from you, when you knew a kind of love was emerging in your heart that was not of this world. It may even happen because one day, for a reason you will never know, you decide to actually listen to the preacher at your door with some ridiculous pamphlet about salvation. Sometimes Jesus gleams unmistakably across a remembered prayer, or a Bible story, and this time you know it is really him. God's hand reaches from eternity and taps you on the shoulder and tells you, gently, to turn around.

When I was in college, a woman in a fiction class came up to me and asked "Do you know Jesus?" I didn't know what to say. I must have said "yes." She said "I could tell from your stories. Can I tell you something?" She went on to tell how, while undergoing surgery a year earlier, she had been overwhelmed with a feeling of being loved, and she said she knew it was Jesus. She had not read the Bible, and had not attended church. And she had not told anyone about this until telling me. My first reaction was "You're crazy! How can you know it was Jesus?" But how could I, or anyone, say that it wasn't? And for a year, she had been following him, reading the New Testament and trying to do what it said. This experience, hazy to me because of its subjectivity, had changed her life. It had a more powerful effect on her than many gospel presentations, with their precise content,

16 *The Beginning of the Gospel*

Our dilemma is whether to take God's hand or not. To follow God, to take his hand, means to let go of the other things that lead us. These are the branches, the things we count on to look good and to feel good about ourselves.

For some of us our branches have five bedrooms and a three-car garage. Some of our branches involve relationships that we depend on, or where we are depended upon like a branch ourselves. We get comfortable. Now we can always try the trick where we hang onto the branch and to God's hand as well, but the end of that is to be torn in two. I have a friend who claims that these are really the most miserable of all people—the half Christians, who are too attached to the world to let go of it, and too attached to God to let go of Him. In that position we never feel good, and nearly always feel a vague or even a strong sense of guilt for disappointing someone, somewhere.

But how do we know God's hand is reliable? That's what the rest of the gospel is meant to show us. Following Jesus, grabbing onto God's hand, is a sure thing. It is the surest thing we will ever have dangled in front of us and offered so gently and so generously.

Jesus steps from eternity onto a page of paper in a Bible you bought, sealed in plastic, perhaps marked down so that some company or store could move more Bibles this month. Jesus appears in Mark's story like a flash. But of course that is always how he appears to us—in a flash. For an instant. We glimpse something brilliant from this book of brilliant things. God whispers his presence to us in a way that is unmistakable.

When I was very young one night just before Christmas I woke up at three or four in the morning, and for some reason went downstairs and sat in front of the Christmas tree. Our home was on a hillside and below it the town glowed all yellow from street lights, and a few cars traced their way home in the darkness. I plugged in the lights on our tree. How old was I? I honestly don't remember. Maybe six or seven. I looked at the nativity scene and then up at the tree, that triangle of light that seemed to soar above me, and just then, at that moment, I knew that God was that's often how it is used or perceived. It means turn around. It means there is hope—something wonderful to turn around to. A Kingdom, a world with God at its center, a world so close it is at hand. All one need do to enter is open that clenched fist a little and turn it, empty, towards God.

It may seem strange that the first thing Jesus does when he opens his mouth is say, "turn around." When does someone tell you with urgency to turn around? This happened to me once when for some reason I wound up driving down a one-way street in the wrong direction. People started shouting and waving and communicating the same imperative—"Turn around!" Why? For my safety. They don't want me to be killed, or to hurt someone else. There's a better, safer, though perhaps slower way to reach the destination.

Another image of repentance comes from Jesus' use of the term "at hand." "Something is at hand that can help us repent and find safety again. Maybe it's literally a hand that is at hand. I think of those *Roadrunner* cartoons, when the coyote, chasing the Roadrunner and not watching very carefully, falls from a cliff. Invariably he gets some temporary relief by grabbing onto a branch on his way down. Then the coyote dangles there, safe but not safe, relieved and afraid at the same time. What does he need? A savior with a strong hand.

The picture of someone hanging by a branch can be a picture of our lives. Maybe the coyote himself is a picture of all of us. We are all chasing something, and it seems to elude us each time we get close. Sometimes it can seem as though we are, like the coyote, chasing something that is smarter, and faster than we are and that does not want to be found by us. We are all suspended—safe for now, but we can't stay that way forever. We are alive, some of us even in fairly pleasant circumstances, but none of us can keep ourselves alive forever. Jesus is God's hand reaching down to save us. He calls over the cliff: "The kingdom of God is at hand." Repentance means letting go of the branch and clasping onto God's hand, so that we can be led and loved by him.

CHAPTER 2

The Beginning of the Gospel: Rescue

> *And passing along the sea of Galilee, he saw Simon and Andrew the brother of Simon casting a net in the sea; for they were fishermen. And Jesus said to them, "Follow me, and I will make you become fishers of men." And immediately they left their nets and followed him. And going on a little farther, he saw James the son of Zebedee and John his brother, who were in their boat mending the nets. And immediately he called them; and they left their father Zebedee in the boat with the hired servants, and followed him.*

Jesus was walking along by the sea, thinking who knows what? Maybe he was thinking tragic thoughts as he began to realize, to sense, the deadly course his life would take. Or perhaps he was delighting himself in the things he noticed that still bore some reflection of God in this world: The love he knew from his human parents. The way, occasionally and so rarely, human beings treated each other kindly. Small things like a word of affirmation from a husband to his wife. Perhaps Jesus saw that and in it saw a clearer picture of God's love for human beings than he would have found in all the public piety of the religious leaders.

Well, whatever he was thinking as he walked along on the shores of the Sea of Galilee, what finally got his attention was a group of young men who were fishing.

Mark tells us that Jesus saw Simon and Andrew and then James and John, and he called them to follow him. But what did he really see? Did he see four boys' hearts, hungry for more out of life, who if they could have pinpointed it would have said in a moment that they were hungry for God? Did he see in them a thirst for a life of adventure, danger, and the truest love they could ever know? And how did he know that they were hungry and thirsty? Did their dissatisfaction show? Were they reckless partiers? Like those of us who have been reckless ourselves have done, did they show their hunger for life every night in the town's bars and bedrooms? Maybe they were hung over that very morning, and maybe they were smoking the day's first cigarettes, hoping to sear their consciences and drive away that uneasy feeling of emptiness. Maybe they knew that the little contentment that they did have was as thin as smoke. Did they seem bored with fishing and envision dull futures—every day the same old thing?

Or did Jesus see nothing? Was this a guess? Did he sense an urging from heaven, and answer to his prayers for guidance, a whisper from the Father that said, excitedly, "These are the ones I told you about"?

What did he see? What does he see in any of us that he should call us and invite us into the greatest of all lives? What did he see in me, that he should extend his hand so many times? When I was in the hospital, just after high school, a religious woman came and told me a bit about Jesus. I listened politely, embarrassed and uncomfortable because I didn't understand a thing she was saying and because a friend was visiting me at the time as well. When the woman left I laughed and made fun of her superstition. My friend turned to me and said with a kind of seriousness that has kept her words in my memory and will probably fix them there forever: "You know, I could see you becoming really religious." She was right, of course, though "religious" is still not a word I'm entirely comfortable with. What did my friend see? Can we see the hunger for God in others but not in ourselves? Was it plain as day to Jesus that morning that these boys were looking for God, searching for the Messiah?

One of the unfortunate things about the gospels is that we're rarely allowed to see what Jesus was thinking to himself. This is of course the cause of a good deal of frustration among theologians. Did Jesus think he was the Son of God? Or did Jesus think he was merely a human teacher and it was his followers who invented the Son of God myth after his death? Or was the Son of God myth invented while he was alive and whoever invented it managed to convince Jesus himself that it was true? And if Jesus was the Son of God, what was it like for him? Did he know it all the time? Did he hear a voice like Luke Skywalker heard the voice of Obi Wan Konobi? Did he learn as he trusted and obeyed that the one who spoke to him was his Father in heaven? Is that what happened at the baptism? As he came out of the water and the Spirit came upon him, did eternity flash through him like lightning and did intimacy with God flood his heart as thoroughly as the river had just overwhelmed his body? Did the pieces of his life fall together like a puzzle and suddenly he saw the picture whole—the past, present and future, so that afterwards he could stand up and say the absurd with confidence: "Time is fulfilled. "Your king has come!"?

Whatever the answer is, we're just not told very much. Perhaps because no one knows or ever knew. Or perhaps because in our pride if we knew, we would find something else to imitate rather than to simply love. In our hearts there seems to be an inclination toward legalism, which has more in common with acting than with real religion. We would rather act the part of the Christian at times, and hope that is enough, rather than go through the struggle of trying to figure out just who Jesus is and what it means to know him and love him. Acting is so much easier. Oh, it takes work to go to church, attend committee meetings, have personal devotions, and to lead a tidy life and abstain from immoral behavior. You can see it takes work because you can see the tiredness of many religious people who grimly carry out their responsibilities, and who grimly advocate their lifestyle. But it is not nealy as difficult as hanging from a cliff, crying out to God and unashamedly expressing our desire for him, and waiting for a response, struggling to see him.

Acting like a Christian is easier than loving God. The actor wants applause at the end, to be told how talented he has been. The lover wants only to know and to be with the one he loves. The lover is unashamedly interested in joy, in a joy that draws all attention to its source. John the Baptist is a great lover of God, a fool for love, dreamily declaring the attributes of the one who is coming, calling all attention to him. Far from coveting applause he defers it, claiming that the one to really praise, the one who will draw us time after time to our feet in worship, is yet to come. "This fellow is so much greater than I am," John tells his followers, "I wouldn't dare even tie his shoes."

Maybe what Jesus saw in those fishermen was their capacity to be great lovers. Perhaps he saw beneath their rugged exteriors, calloused over the years by their disappointments and their mistakes. Under all that maybe Jesus could see their capacity for heart-breaking and heart-filling love. And maybe that is why they followed. Maybe they knew somehow, deep down where you feel things and know things with a kind of certainty that is more reliable than any of the five senses, perhaps they knew that at last they'd found someone worthy of that kind of love.

Perhaps like many of us they'd already tried every version of human love possible, some of it satisfying and some of it devastating, but none of it hinting at the security of the kind of love God offers us. Maybe they'd been reading their Bibles, and when they met Jesus they heard the voice of the rescuer at the cliff that Isaiah had found:

> "I am the Lord your God who takes hold of your right hand and says to you 'Do not fear; I will help you.'"

Perhaps like us they had tried every pleasure that had passed before them, only to find the joy of it slip away like mercury, and feeling in the end, at the very best of times, that maybe, just maybe, real lasting pleasure was around the next corner. Yes, maybe they'd been reading their Bibles, and when Jesus called them they heard in his voice the voice of the rescuer at the cliff that David had found:

> "You have made known to me the path of life, you fill me with joy in your presence, with eternal pleasures at your right hand" (Isa 2).

These boys saw the hand of God extended toward them, and they took it. They took it so immediately and completely that it scares us and makes us uncomfortable. How could they leave their jobs, their families, their futures, all in a moment? How could they drop it all and follow this man who had only spoken two very ordinary words—"follow" and "me." Isn't it too much to expect of anyone, especially me, two thousand years later, and with what feels like two thousand times more responsibility? Jesus appeared to them like a flash and in a flash they were out of their boats and walking with him to . . . who knows where?

Their response seems unreasonable to us, and in a way it is unreasonable. But if we are to use our reason alone, we will never find God. If we live only by reason, we will never do illogical things. We would never trust, be generous, or forgive. That would make us weak, and if reason tells us anything it tells us weakness is bad. By reason alone we would be safe and strong and protect ourselves at all costs. Our reward for this would be that we would feel that we have never made a mistake. We would never take risks. We would never fall in love. We would never hurt, for we would never love and our hearts will never break, for they will harden and shrink into something dark and dense that the writers of the Bible compare to a stone.

It scares us to see an example of immediate, total, exhilarating commitment to Jesus because we don't know if we are capable of making such a commitment, and then we hope we will never be asked to do it. But I think that there is another side of us that is completely unreasonable, that thinks (if we allow ourselves to admit it), "If I were they I would have done the same thing. If I were there, and saw the real Jesus, and knew it was he promising to fill my life with love and security, freedom from fear, if I knew this was really God, right in front of me, I'd go for it." If we really knew it was God who was reaching out to us, we would take his hand.

If you are thinking that, or if you have ever thought that, be prepared. As Jesus says in the Beatitudes, "Happy are you who hunger and thirst for righteousness, for you shall be satisfied"

(Matt 5:6). You shall be satisfied. If you are hungry and thirsty for life, I believe God will come to you and offer his hand. And I believe that you will take it. You will be terrified and you will be thrilled, and you will find yourself letting go of things you never thought you could release. You will find that some people think you're crazy, and others will claim you're doing the sanest thing they've ever seen you do. But most importantly, as you let go of your branch and take God's hand you will find somewhere in the back of your throat a small, small taste of the sweetest most satisfying flavor you have ever known. You will brush against true joy, the real joy that all our substitute pleasures only caricature in a clumsy, comic way. Ambition, any kind of intoxication, the pleasure of wealth, fine things, successful careers, successful children—as wonderful as some of these things can be, they all fade into the background when we open our hearts to God and take his hand. When we take God's hand we touch (lightly) heaven, and because of the thrill of it we will chase it for the rest of our lives.

CHAPTER 3

The Beginning of the Gospel: Faith

> And they went into Capernaum: and immediately on the Sabbath he entered a synagogue and taught. And they were astonished at his teaching, for he taught them as one who had authority, and not as the scribes. And immediately there was in their synagogue a man with an unclean spirit; and he cried out, "What have you to do with us, Jesus of Nazareth? Have you come to destroy us? I know who you are, the Holy One of God." But Jesus rebuked him, saying, "Be silent, and come out of him!" And the unclean spirit, convulsing him and crying with a loud voice, come out of him. And they were all amazed, so that they questioned among themselves saying "What is this? A new teaching! With authority he commands even the unclean spirits, and they obey him." At once his fame spread everywhere throughout all the surrounding region of Galilee.
>
> And immediately he left the synagogue, and he entered the house of Simon and Andrew, with James and John. Now Simon's mother-in-law lay sick with a fever, and immediately they told him of her. And he came and took her by the hand and lifted her up, and the fever left her; and she served them.

We may never know exactly what Jesus saw in people and what he sees in us. But we are allowed to see some of what people saw in him.

It started with John the Baptist. He started talking about someone who would come and unleash the Spirit of God. He told people they needed to be ready, prepared for this, to begin to let go of their branches, to repent. Now I would guess that if you or I were to stand up and start telling people to repent we would find that our names were removed from the invitation lists to most peoples' parties. No one likes to be told that they must change. I doubt that people in John's day, in general, liked to be told what to do any more than we do. But what happened? We are told that people ran out to John by the hundreds and thousands. Why? Was it John's integrity? The genuineness of his joy? Was the Holy Spirit already there, tickling people with a foretaste of what it would be like to be truly and finally filled? Something got through to people and made them want more than anything to be prepared to meet God.

Then when Jesus arrives on the scene, and is baptized, every time he speaks something phenomenal happens. Four fishermen leave everything like lovestruck couples eloping to be with him. He walks into a synagogue and starts teaching in a way that, frankly, blows people away. While he is there a man with an unclean spirit comes and challenges him. What an unclean spirit is and what a man with one is like, are questions to be answered by someone other than myself. A voice from the world of darkness reaches out and seizes the heart of a person and, however it happened, that person belongs to someone other than the one who created him or her. Jesus opens his mouth and the spirit's grip on the man is broken. Then he goes to Simon's home and, as if to contrast the violence of the previous episode, tenderly speaks a fever away. And as if to underline what it means that the kingdom of God is at hand for us who are weary from hanging by branches, he takes the woman by the hand and lifts her into health.

What do people see in Jesus? The first thing they remark about is his authority. He teaches in a way that sets him apart. He speaks and demons flee. He speaks and sickness falls off like a shell, and he nurtures the soft, tender life that is revealed. "What authority!" the people say. Why? Perhaps because in traditional rabbinic teaching, scribes drew their authority from other authorities. Like twentieth-century scholars, you prove your wisdom by demonstrating that you've read and responded to all other scholars on the topic. Jesus, we know from other records of his teaching, footnoted no one. If a scribe would say "Well, Rabbi Jones says this on Psalm 23," Jesus says, "Truly, truly *I* say to you." Whose authority did he defer to? No one's. Who has the authority to speak on a text and say "I know what it means"? The author of course. Others can only claim to have an opinion. Jesus, it seems, talks about Scripture as if he wrote it.

The same thing happens with the unclean spirit. If anyone else were to dare attempt an exorcism, they would certainly do it in God's name, just as Christians who deal in this sort of thing do it in Jesus' name: "In the name of Jesus, I command you, come out." But Jesus defers to no one and simply says "I tell you, come out." It's so unheard of that people speculate that perhaps he's trying to start a new religion. But it's not a new religion. It's not a relgion at all. It is the King himself, the great and terrible day of the Lord. He's here. And the hallmark of a king, what makes him different from everyone else in the kingdom, is his authority. And that is what people notice and are simply stunned by. He teaches Scripture like he wrote it. He commands demons and they obey him. What is this?

What is it indeed, and who was it for? Why all this attention on miracles and healing? Some say that Jesus was flashing his ID to the crowds. He was convincing them of his connection to God with this power display. I doubt it. In most cases he shows little interest in impressing people as an end in itself. Who would be wondering about the extent and nature of his power and authority? Most likely those four boys who had just left everything to be with him. What had they gotten into? I wonder how they felt with each step that they took, each step away from their jobs and families. Did they grow more nervous and afraid? What was to become of them? When they heard this voice something sank into their souls and touched a part of them they'd never dared share with anyone—their deepest desires, their hunger for a spiritual satisfaction that they feared admitting because it would only draw laughter from their friends. Now they were actually acting on it, and with every step they took with Jesus, they came closer to the realization of their dreams but also closer to the possibility of disappointment and with it a deeper pain, disillusionment, and humiliation than they could face if it all turned out to be a farce.

That is you and I walking with Jesus, taking those first few cautious steps, feeling thrilled but also terrified because if it's not true—and how there are times when it seems untrue—if it's not true we will feel and look foolish. But worse than that, we will be devastated if we finally dare admit something as crazy as wanting to know eternal love, and we find it a mirage like all the other pleasures we pursued. What would be left in a world without love?

That summer when I was reading the New Testament, I was hunting for an apartment near campus for the fall. As is the case in most college towns, finding an apartment is extremely difficult. I rode my bicycle to dozens of buildings, always to find that they'd been taken. One night, desperate, tired and frustrated, I decided for some reason to try prayer. I'd never done that before, and I think what I did was promise God that if he'd find me an apartment I'd be his best friend forever. It was more of a bargain than a prayer, I suppose. We always feel like we must do something to deserve God's favor.

The next day I happened to pass by one of the buildings I'd looked at, and the landlord was there, watering the lawn. He saw me and remembered me and flagged me down to tell me that the couple whom he had given the apartment to had not worked out and that I could have it if I was still interested. I stood there and remembered my prayer (not, of course, my promise) and was stunned. Could it be . . . no, I told myself, just a coincidence. Too small a thing to be a miracle.

Did God answer that prayer? Of course. For me it was like taking the first step away from the boat. Reading the Bible for me was like standing at the entrance of this new world and wondering if I should step in at all. The greatest question was "Will it be worth it?" God will show us that it is worth it. He will show us in small ways if that is what is needed, or in spectacular ways if that is what is needed. And that is why Jesus shows his authority after the disciples leave everything to follow him. It's his way of saying he can take care of everything. It's his way of reassuring us as we start to take those first shaky steps to follow him. He knows, I think, how weak we are, and how thin are our promises to stay with him.

Jesus reassures those young fishermen that, having taken God's hand they have put their lives in the surest, strongest grip in the universe. They may still look foolish to their contemporaries, and sometimes they will feel foolish, but they will know deep down that someone strong and loving has got hold of them. Jesus proves his authority to the crowds, yes; and to the spirit world, yes; and to Simon's family, yes. But most of all he proves it to those who have let go the branch. It may be through dramatic things—you may find that your personal demons flee the instant you pray your life into God's hands, things you never thought you'd be free from. Or you may hear in a sermon, or see in a face of a stranger, something small that at once reminds you and reconvinces you of the truth of the love of God. Or you may pray for something and see it come true so literally that it will shock you into slamming the door behind you and entering the kingdom of heaven for good.

It will take a lifetime to be pulled up to the top where the gorgeous terrain of the kingdom is waiting, spread out like a dream, only a dream so real and tangible and tasteable that our life here will seem like an illusion by comparison. And as if to reassure us that we will make it there, someday, through every danger and toil and snare set for us by the world and set for us by ourselves, God makes those first few tugs upward so strong and so thrilling that we long to go the rest of the way.

CHAPTER 4

The Beginning of the Gospel: Love

> *And a leper came to him, beseeching him, and kneeling said to him, "If you will, you can make me clean." Moved with pity, he stretched out his hand and touched him, and said to him, "I will; be clean." And immediately the leprosy left him, and he was made clean. And he sternly charged him and sent him away at once, and said to him, "See that you say nothing to anyone; but go, show yourself to the priest, and offer for your cleansing what Moses commanded, for a proof to the people." But he went out and began to talk freely about it, and to spread the news, so that Jesus could no longer openly enter a town, but was out in the country; and people came to him from every quarter.*

I love this story about the leper. I love it not just because this leper is a picture of all of us. In a way I love this story in spite of its being a useful analogy for human life. I love this story because it is about a real person, a specific individual who lived close to two thousand years ago and I love it because Jesus was moved deeply by this person and so reached out to him.

It's easy for me to think sometimes that Jesus wandered the earth during his life, looking for ways to make good Bible stories. "Here's a leper," he may have thought. "This will provide a useful example of my compassion when the New Testament is written." The reality, of course, is that the incidents recorded for us are great examples of God's love, but that's not why Jesus performed miracles. He is moved with pity. He loves this leper. And he loves us and that is why he will stretch out his hand to heal us when we cry out to him. He heals not to create examples, not to provide us with a testimony, but because he loves us.

That's really what is at the heart of the leper's question to Jesus. It isn't exactly a question at all but more of a statement: "If you will, you can make me clean." A paraphrase might read, "If you want to, you can help me." All that's in question for the leper is whether Jesus wants to help him. Maybe the real question he is asking is, "Do you love me?"

This is one of the most vulnerable and searching things anyone says to Jesus. Each of us must be certain of two things if we are to follow Jesus. One is that he is strong enough to take care of us. The second is that he loves us and wants to take care of us. Sometimes we fail to trust him because we don't think he can help us in a given situation. Other times, and this is the leper's situation, we're confident that Jesus can help us if he wants to, but we struggle to believe that he wants to, that he really loves us.

The leper may have seen or heard about other miracles Jesus had performed. We often see and hear of the same things, whether it's on television or in the lives of our friends. People claim to have put their lives in God's hands and found healing, peace, deliverance from besetting struggles with anything from dieting to drug abuse. You may even see real, lasting change happen in their lives. And so, to a degree, you are convinced that God can change people, transform their lives and bring freedom and joy.

The next question is, "Could he do that for me?" The real question may be "Would he do that for me?" Does he want to? Does God love me? It's often easy to believe that God loves the world. If there is a God and he created the world it would make sense that he loves it. But does that mean he loves me? Does that mean that he will pay attention to me, my problems, large and small, tragic and comic?

Jesus answers the leper's question and ours without hesitating. "Moved with pity, he stretched out his hand and touched him and said 'I will, be clean.'"

"You could heal me if you wanted to," the leper says. "Of course I want to," Jesus says, taking that tired old moth-eaten face in his hands, looking deeply into those fading eyes, "because I love you." This leper, if he's like every other leper of the day, had been forced to wear a bell around his neck, to warn people to flee as he approached. Because leprosy was considered highly contagious, lepers were forced to shout "Unclean! Unclean!" when near other people. In other words this leper had been told all his life that he was worthless, and he had been saying it about himself too, shouting it so everyone could hear. If you're smart, he was essentially telling the world, you'll run away from me. There's nothing but ugliness and decay in this body.

And this is where the story of the leper touches something in each of us, because somewhere, sometimes, we all feel this way about ourselves, and we wonder, is it true? Am I really worthless? Some people seem to like me, but maybe that's just because I dress well or have money or drink with them or sleep with them or take care of them. If people knew what I was really like on the inside, the bad things I've done, the thoughts I've had, they'd run away from me. Maybe they'd put a bell around my neck, too, or just talk about me when I'm not around. Is there anything, deep down, lovely or lovable in me?

We learn to feel like lepers because sometimes we're treated that way. I met a young man whose parents had gotten divorced while he was in school and each had moved to live with their lovers. They left him to live alone in what previously had been their family home. In their minds, the parents were being generous. In his mind, he was worth nothing to either of them.

An overweight person is taunted. Someone is avoided, or, worse, treated with impeccable, distant, politeness, because of their ethnic background. Someone tells us they'll call and never does. These things all raise the same question for us, in small or large ways. At the core, am I worthless? Does any one see any beauty in me?

The question moves Jesus, when he hears it from the leper and when he hears it from us. And he stretches out his hand to touch us in the places where we feel worst about ourselves, and he says, "Of course I see the good in you, the breathtaking image of God in you, the beautiful desperate capacity for love." For us to believe something good about ourselves we must hear it from

God, because God is objective and has standards. He does not lie and he does not flatter. He's not just saying it to make us feel better. When the source of all truth tells us he loves us we know it must be true, and we know a love that is deeper and more reliable than any person could ever give us.

Jesus tells the leper, "Be clean." Several miracles happen at once for this leper. His flesh, shredded by his disease, is restored. Open wounds close up. Calloused, numb extremities soften. Nerves come back to life like wires when the power is switched on, and they transmit sensations through his body in a way that must be thrilling and terrifying. But the greatest miracle, and the greatest miracle that will ever happen to any of us, is that of being made "clean."

Jesus tells the leper to be clean, I think, because he has been made to feel like dirt all his life. He wants him to know that as well as restoring his body Jesus is peeling off the layer of guilt and fear and self-contempt that has covered him for years. Be clean. Know that there is nothing for you to hold against yourself, or for anyone else to hold against you. To make sure no one blames you for anything anymore, go to the priest and have it confirmed. Clean. All our pain scrubbed off. All the doubts about ourselves, our relationships, sprayed away with a touch.

I think most of us would much rather feel clean on the inside than to look good on the outside. We want to know, deep down, that we are loved. We want to worry less about what other people think of us—friends, family, employers, co-workers. We don't want to have our moods and self-perception controlled by other people. And we want to know that when we screw up in the future, cleanness—forgiveness—is as close as Jesus' hand. We want to be free of the crippling fear of failure that makes all of our words and actions come out stillborn with caution and qualifications. Mercy makes us clean. It's something we can't give ourselves. Mercy is available all day every day from God himself, the maker of right and wrong. If Jesus loves us and forgives us we can be a little more daring in our attempts to really live.

To know that kind of cleanness seems impossible. It is certainly impossible to describe with any kind of scientific precision. Blameless is a synonym. I suppose we only really know it when we experience what the leper experienced. Coming to Jesus, wearing our desire like a badge and asking, "Do you love me?" and coming away with our guilt and pain skinned off our backs and replaced with the soft, tender, new flesh made of love and fixed on us with mercy.

The leper was hanging by a shaky old branch and he knew it. He hollered shamelessly for help. When Jesus looked over the cliff the leper said "I know you can pull me up if you want to" and the next thing he knew the strongest grip in the universe was around his wrist and around his heart.

We would all do well to pray this leper's prayer. It's not really a prayer but a statement with an implicit question: "Do love me?" We would all do well to allow God to touch us in the areas of our lives where we feel like dirt. And, of course, we would do well to hear Jesus say, "Of course I love you, be clean from that garbage," and feel things snap back together in our hearts in a way, perhaps, that only we can understand, telling us we are clean and we are loved by the creator of all things.

Jesus touched a leper. This is significant because if there was one thing you weren't supposed to do to lepers it was touch them. That was why they were to warn people of their approach. If you touch a leper you risk contracting the disease. When Jesus touched the leper the opposite happened. Instead of Jesus being infected the leper was healed. There is nothing in us or about us that Jesus cannot touch. There is nothing he is afraid of treating. His love is more powerful than any struggle or sin, and it can wash away the guilt and shame we feel as quickly as it can close the leper's sores. We cannot infect Jesus. If we're lucky he will infect us with a kind of mercy and compassion that will free us not only to be clean but to touch the lepers around us as well.

Jesus is not afraid of our problems, if they are physical, spiritual, or emotional. He is not repulsed by our ugliness, if it is because we are victims or criminals. He is moved with pity and is eager to bring healing. He is eager like the father in the story of the Prodigal Son to throw his arms around us and give us the kind of life we've always wanted. Because he knows that what we've always wanted is not luxury but love. Not riches but richness. Not money but mercy. So when we come to him, dirty and disillusioned, empty and ashamed, wondering if he can possibly love someone as unworthy as we are, he says, "Of course I love you. I have always seen the good in you. Now I can help you close up the evil so you can know what it is to be really human." He will cover our pain with a robe of royalty and like the leper we will find out what it is to really feel things and new sensations will flood our minds and hearts.

The story of the leper is important because he was a real leper. Not a metaphor. Not an illustration. He was a person who came to Jesus with all his fear and desire. And Jesus' guts churned with compassion and affection. This is important because we are all real people, with real fears and desires and problems that don't seem to just go away. And we need to know that Jesus is moved by us as well, full of compassion and affection. We need to know that he will touch us too, and feel along our bodies to find the wounds that need closing, and feel along our hearts to find the wounds that are inside us as well. We need to know that he will stretch out his hand to us before we've finished speaking to him and keep us in his grip for good.

CHAPTER 5

The Beginning of the Gospel: Friendship

> And when he returned to Capernaum after some days, it was reported that he was at home. And many were gathered together, so that there was no longer room for them, not even about the door; and he was preaching the word to them. And they came, bringing to him a paralytic carried by four men. And when they could not get near him because of the crowd, they removed the roof above him; and when they had made an opening, they let down the pallet on which the paralytic lay. And when Jesus saw their faith, he said to the paralytic, "My son, your sins are forgiven." Now some of the scribes were sitting there, questioning in their hearts, "Why does this man speak thus? It is blasphemy! Who can forgive sins but God alone?" And immediately Jesus, perceiving in his spirit that they thus questioned within themselves, said to them "Why do you question thus in your hearts? Which is easier, to say to the paralytic 'Your sins are forgiven,' or to say, 'Rise, take up your pallet, and walk'? But that you may know that the Son of Man has authority on earth to forgive sins"—he said to the paralytic—"I say to you, rise, take up your pallet and go home." And he rose and immediately took up the pallet and went out before them all; so that they were amazed and glorified God, saying "We never saw anything like this!"

If the story of the leper shows us how Jesus loves lepers, the story of the paralytic shows us how, in a way, we are all able to love the lepers and paralytics around us. Jesus reaches out to someone who is locked up in some kind of pain, and he shows how God can even work through us to ruin evil and to restore life.

Four people decide to help their friend. They know they are powerless to solve his problem. The man is paralyzed, his body stiff with sickness. They may have tried other resources for healing the man. They may have brought him to some local medicine man. They may have tried conventional medical cures. They may even have brought him one of those spiritual healers who promises great results if you could summon faith enough to contribute generously to the ministry. Finally, they decide to bring their friend to Jesus. By this time they are desperate.

And by this time Jesus has become famous. In our world of alienation and loneliness, in our world where each of us carries in our hearts a secret emptiness, a sort of shakiness in our guts that is really that question: Is there anything really lovable in me?; in this world when someone is somehow able to offer love and affirmation and is able to give people real, deep attention and affection—that person will be sought after. People rush to be in places where they know they are loved. Many of us very often feel isolated, even when we are busy and important, often even when we are popular. We will always rush to places where we feel affirmed and safe. We rush to someone who pays real attention to us. Someone who really listens and understands. And so people rushed to Jesus, to hear his voice, to feel his touch, and they came away again and again with the brilliant sensation of security. They had taken God's hand and, once assured of his love for them, they knew that they could walk through anything.

We know that the friends of the paralytic were desperate because of what they were willing to do to bring their friend to Jesus. They fought their way through a large crowd with their awkward freight. They climbed a wall and tore a hole in the roof of some stranger's house to get him to Jesus. Then they lowered the paralytic down like rescue workers at the scene of a disaster, gently and urgently swinging this frozen body to where it would find real help.

The rescue workers take this man to the rescuer. They put him in a place where he will have a chance to take Jesus' hand and be pulled up into life and health. That is really all anyone can do for us, and it is all we can do for anyone else. They get more than they were looking for. When he meets the paralytic

Jesus says, "My son, your sins are forgiven." Were the friends who brought the man initially disappointed? Perhaps they thought "We're not looking for vague words of comfort, but real change!" "Your sins are forgiven" may sound to them something like comforting words we search for when speaking to the seriously injured or ill—"Get well soon." It's the kind of thing you say when you feel hopeless and yet some hopeful comment is expected of you. Often we feel the emptiness of such expressions as soon as the words leave our lips or reach our ears—vacant affirmations of a hope that no one really believes.

But Jesus' words did not sound that way to the scribes who were listening nearby. Ever vigilant to protect their doctrine, they heard in Jesus' words "Your sins are forgiven" a claim that only God could make. Because only God has the power and authority to blow sin off our hearts like wind blows dust up from the ground, they assume that this person is not God and is falsely claiming God's power. The Pharisees call it blasphemy. The friends of the paralytic call it a disappointment.

In response, Jesus says, in effect, "OK, if you're not satisfied that I have authority to forgive sin, or that real healing is taking place inside this locked-up board of a body, I'll prove it to you." And he says to the paralytic "Show them the depth of healing that has happened in you. Get up and walk." And so he does and the people there know they've witnessed something spectacular, something it never even entered their minds to conceive of—that God himself is visiting this world, coming in some kind of fantastic disguise. They look at each other and whisper, breathlessly, "We've never even imagined anything like this."

What have they seen? They've seen shriveled, dead muscles swell alive. They've seen life surge through a body that seemed made more of wood than of flesh. They've seen Pinocchio turn human, only not because he told the truth but because he let Jesus tell him the truth and he welcomed it. Often we can believe that all we need to be whole is the removal of some problems—if I had a better job, if I were free from this addiction, if I were physically well, if I had more money, if I got along better with my family, then I would be content; then I could coast for a while and life would be easy. The paralytic received the truth that what he needed more than physical healing was freedom from sin, freedom from that subversive inclination in our hearts to grab anything but God's hand to take care of us. Jesus stretched out his hand to this man and, like those first four followers, the man, as soon as he could move, took it in a moment.

What have they seen? They have seen someone become human, which is what every one of us really needs. Most of us know that the person we are is not the person we would like to be. We know this each time we look back on our lives and for some reason see only the mistakes we've made. We feel that painful longing, wishing that we had done right. We know it each time we lose our grip on love and say something hurtful to someone we care deeply for. There is a hunger inside us for a quality of life. We want things like nobility, integrity, strength of character to be true of us. These are some phrases that represent what we are after. It is a hunger to see some clear realization and actualization of the good in us. We know it is there but it can be so hard sometimes to let it show. So we settle, often, for being less than human, or less than fully alive, dulling our minds and hearts with distractions that we might forget the fact that we know our lives could mean more. Then we look at Jesus and see someone who is always fully human, fully alive, and the good of human life shouts at us in his every word and action. Like the paralytic we see him and, whatever we say in our stupor of surprise, something deep down in us says "yes," and stands up to follow him.

I knew a student who, when I met him, was one of the angriest, most sarcastic people I'd ever met. He criticized everyone, and went to great lengths to brag about his own accomplishments. As you might imagine he wound up friendless before too long.

I saw him later that year and to my surprise he told me he had met God. Then he told me his life's story, more or less. It was a story of life without love. His family ignored him at best, and as worst harassed him about his academic performance. He was never good enough, and always had to convince the world that he was someone. In response he was always trying to prove his greatness to his peers. He would boast about himself, and publicly mock people doing poorly in school. His angry, superior attitude was a wall built from a loveless boyhood. But something happened to this young man that freed him to be human. He told me, "This is the first time I've ever felt it was possible to be loved, whether or not I succeed." The love he experienced enabled him to help others rather than to just put them down. He started to offer, humbly, to help other students with classwork. Perhaps more amazing was that he began to ask for help with things that he didn't understand. And he began, miraculously, to have friends.

All of us can become human. All of us can become the better person that we sense, sometimes only dimly, is in us somewhere. For this to happen we must first welcome the truth that by nature we run away from God to live our half-baked, half-human lives. We trade love for money. We let go of relationships for ambition. We deny conflict instead of seeking forgiveness. And we have suffered for it, hanging from our branch, alone. So when we turn around and run toward God and take his hand and allow him to lead us, we find the same power surge through us, and our hearts, which can seem so locked up and wooden sometimes, suddenly set free. We are set free by the power of God to be whole.

The paralytic, though, is set free in some measure because of his friends. Four people, at least, loved this paralyzed man. Mark tells us that it's when Jesus saw *their* faith, he heals and forgives the paralytic. This means that it was not only the faith of the paralytic that called forth Jesus' love and compassion. How did Jesus see the faith of the others? Most likely in seeing what they were willing to do to bring their friend to him. He saw that they must have tremendous confidence that Jesus is both willing and able to heal this man. They climbed walls, and tore their way through a roof to get to Jesus. They helped this man become whole.

All of us need friends who love us this much. We need friends who will have faith when we don't. We need friends who will carry us to Jesus when we lack the ability or the desire to go to him. When we are immobilized by sins, by fear, or by doubt, someone has to carry us to Jesus and ask him to heal us. We all have the capacity to throw up huge walls between ourselves and God. We isolate ourselves by ways we behave and ways we think, and we learn to construct a private world that feels safe. We may be empty and alone, but if we let no one into this world at least we know no human can harm us. There are walls of indifference, of the fear of looking bad, of the fear of rejection. We need friends who know us and love us and who will climb over the walls and take us to where we will have a chance to take God's hand once again.

At one point in my life I was jobless for several months. I thought it would be easy to find a job, but it wasn't. I thought it would be relaxing to have a lot of free time, but it wasn't. After a few days, I'd wake up each morning feeling useless. I was aimless and depressed, and had no idea what to do about it. This turned out to be one of the best times of my life. Some friends said, "Why don't you come live with us for a while." I did, for two months. The love and attention I received there helped me to rediscover God's love for me in a fresh way. It came through the generosity of my friends. They opened their home, and their lives, to me. They spent time with me, encouraged me, and it helped me to discover that God loved me even at a time when I was unmotivated and unproductive. When I was paralyzed and hopeless, these friends reintroduced me to Jesus. They carried me when I had little resolve. When I had nothing to offer, they offered what they had: their home and their companionship, and through this I found healing.

I had a friend in college who was paralyzed by sin, but not his own sin. His father left the family when my friend was a boy, and my friend grew convinced that if he had been a better son, his father would not have left and his family would still be whole. My friend responded by withdrawing from involvement with people. He rarely spoke, or took any initiative with other people. He told me later he was lonely, but he was also afraid that if he began any kind of relationship he would ruin it and feel worse than lonely. So he built a wall of silence around himself, a wall made from the debris of his broken relationship with his father. Someone invited him to a group of Christians meeting on campus. He never spoke, but people kept inviting him and he kept coming. He kept coming because they made him feel safe and welcomed. His friends saw something good in him and they said so. Eventually he discovered in a very real way that God loved him, and that God was bigger than his problems and bigger than the sins of his father. In the safety of that truth he has learned to share his life with others. And now, by the power of God, he has friends.

We will all have chances to be this kind of friend for someone. We will have chances to bring others to Jesus; people who, for some reason or another, lack the wherewithal to go themselves. We will find that we want the very best for our friends, so we will search for ways to bring them to Jesus so they, too, will have a chance to take his hand. We will be the rescue workers, climbing over scaffolding, scaling the twisted beams and concrete blocks, those barriers made from the wreckage that people often use to protect themselves. We can be the kind of friend that, in spite of the emotional stiffness and apparent deadness of someone we love, stays with them, for there is life in them yet and if we can only get them to Jesus, they will be revived.

I know someone who likes to say that following Jesus means "getting your hands dirty in other peoples' lives." It seems so true in this little story. The paralytic's friends are up to their elbows in dirt. They get involved. They don't just pass by the paralytic, wave a friendly hand, and say, "I sure hope someone takes care of you someday." They know his problem is severe and when they hear of someone whose love is shattering sickness they do what they can for their friend—they bring him to Jesus. It's difficult and costly for them to do so, and so it will always be for all who decide to get their hands dirty.

Love is costly. It involves effort and ultimately it involves suffering. But when our love for someone moves us finally to bring them to Jesus it puts us in a position to experience the love of God, and see it crack like thunder around us and transform not only our friends but ourselves as well. We will find that we, too, become more human, more ourselves, and more alive because we have chosen to be a good friend.

We all know people who are as frozen in their problems as we can be in ours. We can bring people to Jesus and give them a chance to take his hand. We can't take it for them, and we must let them choose. Often we find the paralysis in our families. A child who seems to be rebellious and unresponsive; a parent who is cold and critical; a brother or sister who we can see is painfully dependent on some negative substance or relationship. We have felt that horrible feeling of hopelessness for change. We have had that sinking feeling where any joy in our lives dries up before we can feel it because immediately we think of someone we love who is locked up in pain. When we feel hopeless we can grow depressed. But we can also grow desperate and if we grow desperate enough we may find in our hearts the desire to introduce the people we love to Jesus.

A final thought on this story has to do with why I believe that this incident is all about people coming to life. Mark gives us some visual imagery to help us see what is really going on here.

See what is happening—four men are carrying a board. A man is lying, rigid, on that board. They dig a hole and lower the man down into it. What is this a picture of? It has all the imagery of a funeral. But what they find in the grave is not permanent death but Jesus—something more powerful than sin, more powerful than death. When we meet Jesus we find someone who can free us from our deadly half-humanness and make us whole people, able to do good and be good and love what is good in this world.

When we meet Jesus we find someone who can touch the parts of us that are dead and stiff and we can watch with amazement as they come to life. He can revive our love for a spouse.

He can revive our love for a parent, a brother or a sister. He can revive our ability to trust when we've been hurt. He can revive our ability to be trustworthy when we've betrayed someone. We will find the hard places in our hearts soften like wax under the flame of God's love. And we will find he works in other people through us as we introduce them to that same love. Jesus will see your faith, and he will touch your friends.

CHAPTER 6

The Beginning of the Gospel: Honesty

> *He went out again beside the sea; and all the crowd gathered about him, and he taught them. And as he passed on, he saw Levi the son of Alphaeus sitting at the tax office, and he said to him, "Follow me." And he rose and followed him.*
>
> *And as he sat at the table in his house, many tax collectors and sinners were sitting with Jesus and his disciples; for there were many who followed him. And the scribes of the Pharisees, when they saw that he was eating with sinners and tax collectors, said to his disciples, "Why does he eat with tax collectors and sinners?" And when Jesus heard it, he said to them, "Those who are well have no need of a physician, but those who are sick; I came not to call the righteous, but sinners."*

One of the most damaging misconceptions about the Christian faith that has somehow gotten loose in our time is this: that you must have your "act" together, or that you must be morally flawless, in order to follow Jesus. Nothing could be further from the truth. If there were any doubt, this passage should clear it up. Here Jesus says it as emphatically as he can, "I came not for the righteous, but sinners."

Jesus was criticized by the religious leaders of his day because he spent time with the wrong kinds of people. Here, for instance, he calls a tax collector to follow him, to spend time with him. Now, tax collectors are rarely popular, but in the Jewish culture of the first century it was even worse, because a tax collector was a Jew who worked for the Roman government. This made him a traitor in the eyes of the religious establishment. By the time of Jesus it was a generally agreed-upon idea that a tax collector was someone who could not have access to God or to the religious community.

But Jesus walks right into the tax office and calls Levi. Jesus approaches Levi while he is doing the very thing that most would say keeps him from God—working for the Romans. Levi was sitting in his tax office, probably counting money. By crossing the street to see Levi Jesus breaks a thousand social and religious barriers. And he does it to make one thing clear: there is nothing that can keep us from God. In fact, the things we think keep us from God, well, they don't. There is nothing you or I have ever done, thought, or chosen that will keep Jesus from approaching us and calling us to follow.

What is Levi thinking as he sees this one whom the people are starting to call "holy" walking toward him? Is he thinking, "Oh no, here comes another pious Jew to chew me out about my irreligious behavior?" Has Levi been feeling his lostness and sensing a spiritual sickness in himself but keeping it secret, assuming he's crossed some invisible line that puts him out of God's reach for good? Maybe he's thinking, "I wish someone would give me a chance. I wish someone could see the good in me. I wish someone would help me see the good in myself, draw it out of me, help me act on it." Whatever he's thinking, when he hears Jesus' voice, and feels the love and acceptance in it, the lack of judgment in it, the welcoming in it, he is out of his chair in a minute. Perhaps Levi had let the world convince him that God doesn't love tax collectors. We must never let the world do the same to us.

What are the things you think keep you from God? What are the things you think make it impossible for God to come to you, for Jesus to walk into your office and say "Come with me, I'd like to spend some time together"? Jesus comes to Levi while he is at work, while he is doing the thing that he has become convinced has put him out of God's reach. And suddenly he finds God's hand in front of him.

Maybe you think you've got the wrong kind of life, the wrong kind of relationship, the wrong kind of social or political views, the wrong kind of lifestyle. Maybe you think, "Jesus isn't going to walk into my office, while I'm counting my money. He's too holy for that." Really he's just holy enough. The holiness of Jesus means he is drawn to human life. His holiness does not lead him to avoid people but to enter into our lives and love us. Jesus goes into Levi's office to show Levi that there is nothing he needs to hide. And he will come to us. He will walk into our lives in the areas where we are most afraid or ashamed.

When I was very young a great crisis in my life was failing algebra in the eighth grade. Already at that age I had become convinced, through a variety of influences, that achieving good grades in school was the key to a happy life. Good grades meant the possibility of a good college, which meant happiness and success. The alternative was always implied but rarely articulated. Bad grades meant no college and a ruined life. This was the world from my eighth grade perspective, and I saw myself on plan B, with things getting worse each time I was given an algebra exam.

I didn't tell anyone my fears, least of all my parents. I was afraid they'd be ashamed of me. Over the semester my fear deepened and finally I couldn't keep it hidden any longer. One night, sleepless with anxiety, I came into the kitchen, crying, and spilled the whole tragic story to my mother. What did she do? Scold me? Of course not. She smiled, told me she loved me and it didn't matter so much what happened in algebra, and sent me to bed. I was the happiest little eighth grader in school the next day, because not only was my secret out, but I was set free with the knowledge that my parents' love was not contingent on a flawless performance.

This is a small picture, I think, of what it means that Jesus came for the sick. This is what he wants us to experience. He knows our problems and wants to show us that he loves us anyway. He knows we struggle, he knows our inadequacies, he knows all the dark things about us that we are afraid to let anyone discover. He wants us to admit it so we can find that he loves us anyway, and so we can let him lead us and empower us to change.

Maybe Jesus loves sinners so much because when we admit our problems we are more honest than at any other time. We are more sincere and in a way, more easily loved. Since eighth grade I have become much more skilled at hiding my problems, and much more determined to avoid appearing weak. I remember once, in one of the more difficult times of my life, admitting to a friend all the ways I thought I had failed as a friend, and he told me, "Bill, you're much more lovable when you admit your sins than when you try and hide them."

Our sickness of soul does not keep us out of God's reach. The opposite is true. Jesus is drawn to those who feel heavy hearted at the darkness in the world and in their lives. He takes us as we are. Jesus asks the first disciples to follow him, with no strings attached. He didn't say, "You can follow me if you promise not to smoke." He didn't say, "You can follow me if you promise not to entertain lustful thoughts." He didn't say, "You can follow me as long as you join the right political party." Jesus calls us to follow, as we are, with all our struggles, faults, doubts, fears, and needs. And as we follow we will be changed. What matters is being with him, taking his hand and hanging onto it. He is the one who can take care of us. Like a doctor he knows what we need to get well. His teaching and example are meant not as arbitrary rules but as a prescription for spiritual health.

Not only did Jesus associate with Levi, this tax collector, but he went and had dinner at his house, with all his tax collector friends. "Why is he hanging around those types?" the leaders ask. "They're unclean. They ignore our rules. They don't try very hard to appear righteous."

We all love to find some reason to look down on our neighbor; sometimes we can even twist the loving language of Scripture and of our churches to do it. We like to make fun of how people dress, what color they paint their homes, what kind of car they drive, what school they attend, etc. It's all really a way of trying to convince ourselves that we are superior, and that we should not have to associate with people who are different from us.

I was in a church once where, in the bulletin, there was a notice prohibiting "street-people," in other words homeless beggars, from the church property. This, the bulletin pointed out, was in the interest of protecting the buildings and possessions of the church from people who might be tempted to steal. In another church the Alcoholics Anonymous group was asked to leave because they made a mess and the room smelled of smoke after the meetings. In both cases the message was the same. These kinds of groups don't belong in the church. It's for the righteous, not the sinners.

Jesus has something different to say. He came for the sinners, the sick. Rather than look for reasons to look down on people, he looks for ways to accept them. He walks right into Levi's office, and then he goes to Levi's home. Jesus lets Levi know he is proud to be associated with him. Jesus loves sinners, and thank heaven he does. He comes for those of us who have problems and know it. He comes for those of us who haven't been trying too hard to play by religious rules. He comes for those of us who may look unrighteous on the outside, but on the inside we find in our hearts some hunger for truth and beauty and fullness in our lives. He comes for those of us who know we are at best half-human and half-pleased with ourselves. And he will come to us in the midst of our struggles, to our offices and to our homes, to show us that he is not ashamed of us. He accepts us, and invites us to follow him.

Jesus compares himself to a doctor and explains by way of this analogy what he means. Just as a doctor comes for the physically sick, so does Jesus come for the spiritually sick. You don't have to have your act together. In fact, those who consider themselves righteous are the ones who have the hardest time coming to terms with Jesus. Self-righteousness is a liability. Sickness, neediness, a sense of incompletion, failure, and even rebellion are not liabilities. They are more like prerequisites to knowing Jesus.

Jesus loves sinners. "Sinner" is, of course, an unpopular word in our culture as it has been parodied and caricatured to death. But sin, defined as spiritual illness, is what we all struggle with. Being spiritually sick is like being physically sick. When someone hits us too hard our ribs will break. When someone we love rejects us, our hearts will break. A stroke can make it so that your limbs don't respond to your brain. You try to lift your hand and nothing happens. Sin makes it so that even when we want to do right, we do wrong. We want to say a loving word to a spouse, but we pick at their faults instead.

Medical experts tell us our bodies can do extraordinary things. They can fight deadly diseases, and they can endure extreme conditions. People live through blizzards and live to tell about what should have been fatal accidents. Yet sickness can weaken our bodies to the point where it is difficult even to stand up.

The Bible tells us, too, that we are meant to live extraordinary lives, lives of intense pleasure, heroic sacrifice, and wonderful relationships. Sin interferes. Instead of being heroic we are petty and self-centered much of the time. We struggle to be faithful husbands and wives, children and parents, friends, workers, clients, etc. And we fail so consistently. We take shortcuts, and we cheat. We lie to make ourselves look better than we are. We betray one another, we talk behind each other's backs, we hope for the failure of others to make ourselves look better. It's not because we're evil that we do these things. It's because we're sinful. We sin. And Jesus loves us.

Several years ago I spent a summer in India, and visited Mother Teresa's home for the dying. This is a place where, basically, they bring people off the street who are dying so they won't have to die alone. The Sisters of Charity believe that human life is precious, and that no one created in God's image should suffer the indignity of a lonely, loveless death. So each morning they comb the streets, looking for the poorest of the poor, for those who are starving to death, alone.

I met an American doctor who was volunteering there. He said he had always been suspicious of religion. In fact he was quite frank about having rebelled against his Christian upbringing. But he said he had gotten tired of his life, and he wanted to find out if there was a God. So he came to India to try and "do good," as he called it.

He showed me around. There were rooms full of frail, dying people, some of them so thin that their flesh seemed stretched around their bones like cellophane. There was a walk-in refrigeration room full of dead bodies zipped up in canvas bags. An ambulance came hourly to carry the corpses away. This doctor described the constant suffering that he saw and experienced. Because of the needs he got very little sleep. Because of the discipline of the brothers and sisters he slept in a small, bare room, and lived on a diet of vegetables.

He talked on and on enthusiastically about his work. Most of what he did had little effect in terms of physical healing. They just tried to help people die happy and loved. I could sense real joy in his voice. After a while I asked what kept him going in this difficult life. "Oh," he said. "It's not hard. I love it here." I asked him why. He looked around to see if anyone might hear him, and then he looked at me very seriously and said in a hushed, excited voice, like he was telling me a wonderful secret: "I see God everywhere in this place!"

Here was someone who had admitted the emptiness in his life. He wanted more than success as a doctor. He was honest about his need, and he found God offering his hand. He made no pretensions to be holy, and he came to India with no plan and no answers. But he knew he was sick, and he admitted it, and God appeared. As with Levi, God came into this man's office, and found him through his profession as a doctor.

We must not be afraid of bringing our struggles to Jesus. One of the brilliant things about the gospels is that in all the encounters people have with Jesus, no one seems afraid of him. The most notorious sinners long to meet him, and the weak ones who have suffered injustice or cruelty rush to him when he is near. No one is afraid of him. Why? Because he doesn't prey on weakness. He heals it. He doesn't lecture about how we should have lived, but he welcomes us into the family of God, like the father in the story of the prodigal son, saying only "I'm so glad you're home!" He doesn't look for reasons to criticize us but for ways to draw us into his life.

This should be good news for those of us who spend a good deal of our time feeling guilty about things we've done wrong, or wondering if we should feel guilty. Shame is one of the most destructive emotions that exists. Jesus does not say, "You should be ashamed of yourself." He says, "My child, your sins are forgiven." Shame eats away at us. The only thing worse, perhaps, is what we use to hide our shame, self-protection. Shame is destructive because it makes us hopeless about ever changing. If we believe there is something in the core of us that is reprehensible, we will never ask for help. Self-protection is what happens when, feeling ashamed, we act prouder still, hoping that we can fool the world and maybe even fool ourselves that we really are proud of everything we've ever been. But the more we act, the more difficult it will be to ever admit the pain and the questioning that goes on in us.

Why did Levi follow Jesus? Was he feeling guilty about being a tax collector? Perhaps. Or maybe he was just like a lot of us, unsure about so many things in his life; unsure about how to be faithful to the God of his people and at the same time make a living; unsure about how to respond to being rejected by the religious leaders; unsure about why he made the choices he did in his life; unsure about how to change. Levi was honest. Jesus accepted him, invited him to join him, and had dinner at his house.

We all need to be able to admit our sickness of soul. We must be able to be honest about the ways we have failed, the things we don't understand, and the things that we want but can't seem to find. There is nothing wrong with coming to God and saying, "I want to be happy." That's why Jesus uses the analogy of the doctor, for why would anyone come to a doctor other than with the simple wish, "I want to be well." We all want happiness. We want truth, beauty, joy, and peace. We want to be able to love and to know that we are loved. The problem lies not in our desires, but in what we turn to in order to satisfy those desires. Jesus is thrilled when sinners quit chasing fleeting, deceptive pleasures and come to him.

God will walk into your office. He will walk into your kitchen, your bedroom, your swimming pool, wherever it is that you're most unsure of yourself. Because he wants you to know that nothing can keep him from you. He'll come to your home for dinner. Jesus is not out to give people a list of rules to follow. He wants to share life with us. He's interested in relationship, a relationship of such pleasure and assurance of love that it heals us of all sin and shame and sickness and leads us to health.

CHAPTER 7

Conclusion

Novelist Walker Percy points out in his book *Lost in the Cosmos* that, basically, we are all consistently alienated from ourselves. "Why is it possible," Percy asks, "to learn more in ten minutes about the Crab Nebula in Taurus, which is 6,000 light-years away, than you presently know about yourself, even though you've been stuck with yourself all your life?"

His point is that there is so much we can claim to know with so much certainty. We are confident about scientific and economic truths. Two plus two equals four. A penny saved is a penny earned. We are sure of many things. Yet we struggle to know our own hearts' desires. Will I be happy if I take this job? Will I be happy in this marriage? Will I be happy if I move away from home? Answers to these kinds of questions can be difficult. We struggle to know ourselves, and we agonize over decisions. We are lost in the cosmos, surrounded by more and more scientific certitude, and growing more confused about ourselves each day.

We are lost. I have taken an absurd number of what are called "personality inventories." They are tests that ask you to answer many personal questions and then try and tell you what kind of person you are and what kind of work you will find most fulfilling. Why do I take these tests? Because I can't figure it out on my own. I don't know my own heart well enough. I can't put a finger on what I truly enjoy, what I can live without, what I cannot live without. And each time I take one of these tests, I hope that it will magically chase away the fog and guide me into the bright light of assurance.

They never do, of course. Oh, some things can be learned that are very helpful, but ultimately the problem is that we are lost not from an occupation but from ourselves. A vocational test may tell us some things, but it will not apprehend our hearts and explain them to us. We are lost from ourselves. We are sick. We are sinners, and our attempts to find our way often leave us feeling more hopelessly isolated.

We are lost. I've been lost on camping trips, and I've been lost on driving trips, and I know what happens when I try to find my way back by myself. I get more lost. Once I was trying to drive to Massachusetts from Connecticut (due north). I wound up in New York (due west). I knew I was lost long before I reached New York, but I was too embarrassed to stop and ask for help. So I became more and more lost.

We are lost in the cosmos. We are at sea, living on a tiny bubble of oxygen in an infinite universe, feeling our way through the dark, following dreams we have for ourselves, or perhaps following dreams other people have for us, trying to trace out the shape of happiness and joy. And we have all felt the shattering pain that comes when our dreams disappoint us. We get what we want and it isn't enough. Or we get what we want and it hurts us instead of helping us—the boyfriend or girlfriend, the job, the marriage, the children, the house—whatever we set our hearts on does not shed enough light in our lives to chase out the darkness, the shady feeling that we are meant for more.

We need to find our way home. Home is where we can be ourselves and be comfortable. Home is where we know who we are, where we belong, and where we know what to do. Home is where we know what we want and what will make us happy. Our homes have been broken, split, separated by distance or divorce, but our real home that will tell us everything, put us back together and repair our fractured lives, is with God.

God sent Jesus to show us the way home. The way home is hard in many ways. It has to do with love, suffering, and laying down our lives for others. Jesus shows us everything it means to be human, all the goodness and glory of human life reaches its fullness in him. Ultimately, he gives us power to become fully human by taking on himself our sin. He suffers in our place and we are able to become human and whole instead of staying sick and lost. He shows us the way to God, and finding God has more to do with love and mercy, with generosity and joy, with beauty and peace, than it has to do with legal rectitude and moral precision.

I said earlier that the Bible is like a map that shows us how to find our way home, and so it is. And a map is exactly what a lost person needs. The map will be useful only if we admit that we are lost. We must not be embarrassed or ashamed about asking for help.

I suppose the one other thing that must be true before we use this map is that we must want to go where it leads us. We must have some desire to find God. We must have a thirst for what the Bible calls glory. Glory is all that God is—all the love, goodness, beauty, joy, and freedom exploding around us and inside us. It is not piety, but pleasure. It is not doctrine, but delight. It is the display and apprehension of all that God is and all that he offers us. By apprehension I mean that glory is not something we just learn about or acknowledge. It's something we're meant to experience. It's something we're meant to enjoy. Here's what one person, King David, said of God's glory:

> "I have seen you in the sanctuary and beheld your power and your glory. Because your love is better than life . . . I will praise you as long as I live" (Psalm 63).

David caught a glimpse of God and was lovestruck. He experienced a fragment of God's glory and was stunned. And his conclusion was that the love of God is better than life. The love of God is something so fantastic that he would rather die than lose it. David followed the map and found his way to the treasure, and in finding God found himself. David found out what his life was for, and how he could find the deepest, most lasting pleasure in the universe. Like a fool in love, David went on to seek

God with a kind of lavish, beautiful recklessness. David is the one who fought Goliath with a slingshot. He's the one who was so thrilled to be in the presence of God that he danced before the Lord in his underwear, something so reckless that it embarrassed his wife. David was crazy with love because he found the love that was better than life.

So did John the Baptist, so did the disciples, so did the leper, so did the paralytic and his friends, so did Levi, and the host of sinners. They did the absurd. They dropped everything to be with the one whose love is better than life. They could tell just from being around Jesus that he was that one. And they, too, went crazy with joy.

They knew they were lost, and when they found Jesus they found home. Nothing could tear them away again. All of the first followers of Jesus eventually were killed because of their association with him. John the Baptist went and told King Herod that he should repent. Simon Peter was in all likelihood killed by the Roman Emperor Nero. Their lives, and deaths, are testimonies that indeed they did find love that they counted better than life. Better to lose your life, and keep Jesus, than to keep your life on earth, and lose the eternal, breathtaking love of God.

We have talked about our lostness in many ways, and have used several metaphors. It's like hanging from a branch. It's like being sick and needing a doctor. The Bible calls it sin. We are lost, and once we catch sight of God and see our destination, once we experience a small splinter of God's glory spinning off of some prayer, some touch of love, some word from Scripture or from a sermon, we will grab the map and hang on to it for life.

When we experience God, we will hang onto him like a sick person hangs on to a doctor. When I was in high school, I was in a water-skiing accident that ruptured my kidney. I didn't know what had happened. I only knew that the pain was so acute that I seriously thought I might die. The lake where we had been skiing was an hour from the hospital. So I waited, longing for the first time in my life for a doctor. A doctor represented help—someone who knew what was wrong, and could heal what was hurting. And when I arrived at the hospital I eagerly and desperately did all that the doctor advised me to do.

There are times when we feel the same way about our spiritual lives. "I don't want to feel this way anymore," we'll scream to ourselves. "I don't want to do this anymore," we'll shout when we do something we know we'll regret. And we try to change by willpower, by making resolutions, by taking personality inventories. But we need someone who can heal us on the inside. When we really want this kind of help, we will welcome it when it arrives.

If only we found it easier to admit our hunger for more in life. Not more money, more possessions, or more status, but more joy. If only we found it easier to admit our lostness, our sickness, and our sin. If we could admit that we were hanging from a cliff we would shout like crazy for help, and when Jesus reached out to us like a life line we would take his hand in a flash.

When I was in college, I took a course on comparative religion. On the first day of the class, the professor told us why he thought studying religion is a good idea. He told a story about a certain wise teacher who was sitting beside a stream. One of his students approached him and asked, impatiently, "Master, when will I know God?" The teacher quickly grabbed the student by the back of the neck and shoved his head into the stream, and held it there for an uncomfortable amount of time. Finally, the teacher let go and the student yanked his head out of the water and drew in a long, desperate breath of air. "You will find God," the teacher said, "when you want God as much as you wanted that breath."

May we all desire God intensely and desperately. And may we never be afraid to admit our lostness and our longing, that we might experience for ourselves the beginning of the Gospel. Then we can move from Mark's story of Jesus to our own stories of Jesus.

DATE DUE			
MAR 0 4 1993			
MAY 26 1993			
APR 30 1994			
FEB 1 0 1999			
DEC 1 7 1999			

HIGHSMITH 45-220

Poems by One of Mamie Zarley's Boys

Donald H. Zarley

VANTAGE PRESS
New York

Cover design by Kim Zarley

FIRST EDITION

All rights reserved, including the right of
reproduction in whole or in part in any form.

Copyright © 2002 by Donald H. Zarley

Published by Vantage Press, Inc.
516 West 34th Street, New York, New York 10001

Manufactured in the United States of America
ISBN: 0-533-13960-0

Library of Congress Catalog Card No.: 01-130524

0 9 8 7 6 5 4 3 2 1

To Mamie Ruth and Ray Emerson Zarley

Mamie Zarley
(1897–1990)

I love you, Mother, I love you true;
I'll always be with you when you are blue,
And forever I'll always say,
Be with your Mother on Mother's Day.

(1941)

Contents

Preface ... xi

Chopping Wood on Saturday Morn	1
The Yellow Door	2
Plight of the City Farmer	3
October	5
Futility	6
Jackhammer	8
Down to Aunt Ethel's and Uncle Ed's	9
Belated Greetings	10
Ashes to Ashes	11
The Bully	12
Simple Game, Golf	15
The Early Bird	16
Hospital Boredom	17
Barbed Wire	18
Old Fire Horses	19
Christmas Stocking	20
Old Ned	21
Geriatrics Tool	22
The Funeral	23
Old Age	25
On Stocking Caps	26
Mr. Dow and Mr. Jones	27
Avoiding the Question	28
New History Teacher	29
A Girl Named Alexander	30
Road Rage	31

Ray E. Zarley	32
Brennan	33
Good Listener	34
Making Bread with Flour Green	35
Christmas Greetings in Latin	36
Dixie Christmas	37
A Young Boy's Perception of a Wrigley Field Event	39
Why Do I Give?	41
Marilyn	42
The Midnight of Eternity	43
The Church Office and Indispensible Doris	48
Poet's Lament	50

Preface

First, the title. Yes, I *am* one of Mamie Zarley's boys. (She had four boys, to be correct.) I am also one of Ray Zarley's boys. So why the title? Well, it has a lilt that appeals to me. It raises a bit of curiosity and also has a touch of flattery, because Mamie Zarley was a well-respected woman. It is likely an answer that Jo Beck, a lady across the street when I was young, might have given if asked, "Who is that kid?" Answer: "Oh, he's one of Mamie Zarley's boys." I never heard her say that, but it is just something I could hear her say. So, don't try to read too much into the title. It is at least a tribute to my mother. If I ever have the opportunity to knock on Heaven's door, I will introduce myself by saying: "My name is Don. I'm one of Mamie Zarley's boys." It will put me in good stead.

My very first poem was written to my Mother just before Mother's Day in 1941, when I was in sixth grade. Poems gradually got a grip on me and since then have seemed to bubble forth from time to time. Poetry struck me as a way of saying something in a more profound way than in ordinary conversation. Its subtleties, its power, its descriptiveness, its cleverness seemed to provide a different and higher level of communication. Except for occasionally being asked to write a poem, I never sat down and intentionally wrote one. But ideas would occasionally pass through my mind—a line or two, or even a word or two attached to the filament of an idea, and the poetic seizure would set in. Some would flood my mind at once; others would be ground out, word by word over a long time.

Sometimes the title would be the point of beginning, or the best part of the poem. Sometimes the event or cause of the poem being written was more interesting and entertaining than the poem itself.

There aren't many parables in this collection. No reader or group of students will ever debate over the layers of meaning that the poet may have intended. They are all mostly straightforward. So it is with the unskilled who venture vicariously into the valley of verse. But with all of that is a thread of intellectual honesty and emotion to which at least some can relate. I hope that there is at least one verse or line herein that is just for you.

Poems by One of Mamie Zarley's Boys

Chopping Wood on Saturday Morn

Chopping wood on Saturday morn,
Behind the house where I was born,
In the fall of the year it fell to me,
To split the board and chop the tree.
I loved that job, I don't know why,
But as the sun rose in the sky,
And warmed my body stiff and sore,
From the football game the night before,
The smell of the wood, and fall in the air,
Made it awfully peaceful there,
Except for the ax, hardly a sound,
But for a rooster strutting around,
Crowing at me as if to proclaim,
I was in his private domain,
A time to think, to savor more,
Every play of the night before,
A time to reflect, a time to scheme,
And dream the dreams that young boys dream.
But now the years have come and gone,
Life has changed, and time moves on,
But every year when fall rolls 'round,
And frost comes in across the ground,
I smell the smell of new cut wood,
The memories flow and well they should,
I seem to hear a rooster crow,
And feel the sun and sense its glow.
I see the box with kindling in,
And wish that I could once again,
Chop some wood on Saturday morn,
Behind the house where I was born.

(1991)

The Yellow Door

We had a nice home and a lower floor
With an exit having a yellow door,
And every night as I went to bed,
I grimaced as my father said,
"Good night, Son, and forever more,
Be sure to lock the yellow door."
So for many years I paid my due
And locked that door till my face turned blue.
The years have passed and I am grown,
And trying to build a home of my own,
The roof will be red, the shutters green,
The prettiest place you've ever seen,
But it won't have (I'm a stubborn fellow),
An exit door that's colored yellow.

(1993)

Plight of the City Farmer
(The Firm and the Farm)

The work at the firm, like it or not,
Brings in the bucks, that helps a lot,
The work at the farm, it's fun and thrills,
Won't bring in the dollars to pay off the bills.
(It's not fun to be flat at the farm.)

Back at the firm I sit at my desk
And put on weight and strain my vest;
But at the farm, sweaty and trim,
Hard as nails, with vigor and vim.
(It's fun to be fit at the farm.)

The deals at the firm must come to a vote,
A solo decision will make you a goat,
But at the farm, I beller and boast;
I move the hogs from pillar to post,
I change the plans without alarm.
(It's fun to be firm at the farm.)

The moments in town are priceless gems,
We count them, and keep them, and gather them in,
But at the farm, I fiddle around,
Check the clock when the sun goes down.
(It's fun to be free at the farm.)

There must be a way to join the two;
The best of both worlds, that's what to do,
The bucks at the firm, the fun at the farm,
Would I be willing? (I'd give my right arm
To just move the firm to the farm.)

(1990)

October

Months fly by, October's here!
As summer by us sped.
And now it's almost winter,
Time for trees to go to bed.

Observe the royal beauty
Of the woodlands, golden brown,
It's nature's touch of painting
Over river, field, and town.

The songbird leaves her summer home,
Down South she speeds on wing,
While squirrels stay behind and work
For winter stores to bring.

A Spanish sailor in this month
In fourteen ninety-two
Was first to gaze upon this land
And marveled just as you.

October has another thrill
Besides its gorgeous scenes,
When witches fly and black cats scowl,
You guessed it, Halloween!

October is the time of year
When summer's heat has gone,
And as it closes up the door,
It serves as winter's dawn.

(1945)

Futility

Alone in a waterfront bar room, the swaggering seaman
    was home—
Away from his ship, away from the sea, back in his
    port—but alone.
Mind and soul tortured by reckless living—men's lives
    plundered, hearts left bleeding—
And there he sat, face buried in his hands between each
    drink,
Oblivious of the boisterous laughter of his shipmates—
Boisterous laughter from salty lungs,
Curses and threats from thickened tongues,
Lonely memories only visible, now
Painted on the background of lazy smoke and dim light.
The roll of the ivories sobered his cloudy mind as
The barkeep with the pistol-whipped face presented the
    dancer—
Light-footed, dark-skinned Latin-bred girl—
Lithe body, half naked—each tiny muscle weaving and
    writhing to the strains
Of music being transformed by deft fingers from
    intoxicated mind to intoxicated ears.
Her hands and arms swept the air—up, down, about—
Pulsing, catlike movements—hypnotizing effect—
The toss of her beautiful head—threading of coal-black
    hair over bare shoulder.
The music stopped and she stood near his table and for an
    instant
Their eyes met—for one precious moment the curtain fell
On the past—light perforated loneliness—an oasis
    loomed—
But, like a whiplash, the blow fell as her thin lips
Curled and her dark eyes flashed,

"Bestango, Senor!"—and she was gone—
And again there was nothing but the smoke—
Dull light—the smell of rum—and violent perfume.

(1952)

Jackhammer

Here is a hammer for all kinds of labors
That'll do odd jobs or loan out to neighbors,
It'll cuss you right back whenever you're cussin'
Or drive home a point that your family's discussin'.
And when the time comes for your bungalow for two,
Go right to work and when you're through,
Take this hammer, then worn to the hilt,
And say: "This is the house that Jackson built!"

(1946)

Down to Aunt Ethel's and Uncle Ed's

Down to Aunt Ethel's and Uncle Ed's,
Off like the wind to the pony shed;
There stands Midget all bridled and tied,
Patiently waiting and ready to ride,
Then after a turn, a dash we made
For an ice-cold drink in the cool of the shade,
From the rusty old well at the end of the walk,
By the garden gate and the hollyhocks.
The cyclone cellar was a pirate cave,
Then off to the barn where the kittens played.
Dinner meant Southern fried chicken delight
With all of the trimmings that little boys like,
And home-made bread with a tang of yeast
From the wood-stoked stove, and then at least
A chocolate cake, or to thrill the soul,
Ice cream served in pink glass bowls.
And while we savored this treat of all,
Dan Patch watched from his frame on the wall,
(I was just six, very young then, of course,
But it seemed rather strange for the name of a horse),
Oh, my dear children, so much you have had,
Much more it seems than when I was a lad,
A trip to the mountains, a time at the sea,
So exciting for you, and delightful for me,
But oh, that you had just one trip instead,
Down to Aunt Ethel's and Uncle Ed's.

(1965)

Belated Greetings

Your birthday went by unnoticed,
Though you remembered mine;
Nothing from me at Easter,
And of course, no Valentine;
St. Patrick's Day was a total loss;
What happened to Labor Day?
I meant to send you a Spanish flag
Back on Columbus Day,
So here is small remembrance;
I know not what else to do;
It's for those days that just slipped by,
Oh, yes, Merry Christmas, too.

(1955)

Ashes to Ashes

I could tell you that this ashtray of unique and rare design
Was used by Pharaoh's daughter in a very ancient time,
Or that it's ultra-modern, the very latest thing,
Or F.D.R. had used it in the year he ran for King.

You're wondering why this ashtray is given you by me,
I simply do not want it, you'll understand that, for you
    see,
I won it in a raffle, it must have been a joke!
It's cheap and unattractive, and besides that, I don't
    smoke!

(1955)

The Bully

Dick was seven and I was ten,
We'd always been the best of friends,
He came to me, I'm not sure why,
For in his class there was this guy,
Who bothered Dick, and messed around,
And seemed to put the small kids down.

Dick asked of me, "Endure the flak,
And get this bully off my back,"
I said "O.K." and set about
To get this tough kid straightened out.
I kept my word, and on my own,
I said to him, "Leave Dick alone."

Tom Parnelli was bigger than me,
But with two flunks, his grade was three;
As streetwise Tom sized up his prey,
He knew that I would make his day,
My bark was greater than my bite,
So Tom Parnelli chose to fight.

How could helping the boy next door
Wind up causing a schoolyard war?
But off to the rear of the old school ground
Where Tommy Parnelli would put me down,
A place where I had been before
To watch the school toughs show their gore.

But only to watch, without much fright,
Now I was the one who was scheduled to fight.
My knuckles I had never bared
And I was really very scared.
Impulsively I saw a way,
Just any means to save the day.

Before the crowd, and in disgrace,
I called on him, resolve the case
Without our fists, and walked away
To settle the matter another day.
I trudged on home with head hung low,
Humiliated by my foe.

The mission for Dick had failed somehow,
And Tom Parnelli owned me now.
He taunted me in the following days,
And threatened to get me in several ways,
And finally buoyed by power and might,
He challenged me to another fight.

So back we went where we were before,
A small crowd gathered to watch the score.
We faced each other with fists raised high,
And sensed the moment when blows should fly.
Weeks of anger, frustration, disgrace,
Churned in my bosom on seeing his face.

I hit him, and hit him, and hit him again,
In seconds it ended, it ended for him;
He backed away quickly, his hands dropping low,
He lost his big battle, never landing a blow.

I never was proud of the battle that day,
But the cloud of disgrace had sure gone away;
My memory of Tommy thereafter grows dim,
But he never tormented young Dickey again.

(1996)

Simple Game, Golf

I'm an amateur's amateur—golf is my game,
I play for the fun, and not for the fame;
My score won't compare with the pro's, those fools,
So why should I play with the very same rules?
I concede all putts five feet and less,
Never play a bad lie and get in a mess,
And when I claim a par for me,
I've gotten a par—plus two or three,
When I lose a ball across the tracks,
It comes off my score and my income tax.
You top an approach and then blow a fuse;
I play a new ball with the rules that I use.
But there's one catch to my system, it's true,
My golfing companions are really quite few.

(1952)

The Early Bird

The early bird, it gets the worm, I heard my father say,
And so for, lo these many years from early in the day
Till late at night, I've toiled the whole day through,
And I've got worms, like Father said, and also ulcers, too.

(1962)

Hospital Boredom

There's not much to do while lying in bed,
You can look at the ceiling or stare straight ahead.
If watching paint dry will bore you to tears,
Then try watching paint that's been dry for years.

(1995)

Barbed Wire

Loved by some, or hated like sin,
It keeps things out or keeps things in,
Hard to handle, mean as hell,
Tears your clothes and makes you yell,
Partial to none, you need to know,
It cuts the hands of friend or foe;
It strikes real quick to rip your britches
Or open a wound worth twenty stitches;
Each roll has a mind of its own
To whip you or trip you or leave you alone,
But whether a foe or whether a friend,
It keeps things out, or it keeps things in.

(1998)

Old Fire Horses

Old fire horses, I've been told by folk,
Never lose their excitement at the smell of smoke,
But if I were a horse who had lost its hue,
I'd get more excited at the odor of glue.

(1960)

Christmas Stocking

You think you're pretty smart, you old rascal you,
With a birthday before Christmas, your holidays are two;
A gift each day you will expect, it's simply bound to be,
A gift each day you will receive from everyone but me;
This stocking goes on starboard, (to a sailor that means
    "right")
And the left one, my dear brother, you will get on
    Christmas night.

(1951)

Old Ned

They say he died with his boots on;
That's really not much to say,
So what did they mean by saying that
As they thought of his final day?

Most folks his age are almost done,
Living each day as their last,
Nothing much to look forward to,
And they borrow big on the past,

But old Ned loved the life that he lived,
And he was still going strong,
Without much thought of slowing down,
Or worrying when he'd be gone,

Working not playing was his best game,
For working was play for him;
Helping folks out and minding the store
Was pleasure full to the brim,

The end came quick, not any good-byes,
But like the words in a song,
He lived like he loved, and died like he lived,
And both of his boots were on.

(2000)

Geriatrics Tool

As you rummage through your toolbox,
Is it hard to find the size
Of the wrench that you are needing
Because your failing eyes
Can't focus on the numbers
Emblazoned on the tools?
You guess, and bruise your knuckles,
And wished you knew the rules.

The Commission on the Aging
Has opened up a school
And developed for the old folks,
A geriatrics tool;
You'll have no trouble using it,
So set your mind to rest;
They tried it on some monkeys,
And they all passed the test.

(1982)

The Funeral

I went to a funeral the other day,
It was a sad affair;
All the folks was dressed in black
And everyone was there.
The coffin was a honey—
Purple lining, all complete
With candles burning
At the head and at the feet.
And the organ, it was playin'
Soft music, sad and weird,
An' all the folks was poker-faced—
An' the kiddies, they was skeered!

Then the preacher started talkin'
'Bout goin' to the grave;
He said it wasn't bad
If you hadn't misbehaved;
An' then with teardrops in his eyes
He pointed to the coffin
And said that this soul hadn't died
Because he'd sinned too often;
But some folks raised their eyebrows
As if they didn't believe,
And though they was sober as judges,
They was laughing up their sleeves.

Then came the saddest part of all
When folks all took their feet
An' the preacher said a little prayer
Before he took his seat;
An' then so's folks' kin tell
What they look like when they die,
They opened up the coffin
And everyone passed by,
And the women, they was weepin'
And even menfolk cried,
An' had I known it'd be so sad,
I never would have died!

(1946)

Old Age

When your arteries get hard
And your limbs get old
And your blood gets thin
And your feet get cold
And your hair turns gray
And your joints all creak
And your general outlook
Is mostly downbeat,
Don't be discouraged
Or look with a frown—
Somehow this poem is getting me down.

(1943)

On Stocking Caps

This thing on my head is an odd-looking wrap;
It's not an old sack, but my new stocking cap;
I haven't gone high-hat or got the big head,
And it isn't a night cap to wear when in bed,
But in time of embarrassment, fear or disgrace,
I make like an ostrich and cover my face.

(1946)

Mr. Dow and Mr. Jones

My fortune is controlled,
I've come to realize,
By Mr. Dow and Mr. Jones,
A couple of average guys.

I asked my broker of them;
He shook his head and frowned;
"They're just like all the rest of us,
They have their ups and downs."

So, I write them every Monday,
But I never get replies,
From Mr. Dow and Mr. Jones,
A couple of average guys.

(1997)

Avoiding the Question

While traveling down to South St. Ives,
I met a man with seven wives,
"Why is it, sir, your wives are seven?"
"My eighth one died and went to heaven."

(1955)

New History Teacher

We had Mrs. Clampitt,
We thought we could fool her,
But now she's gone
And we've got Prof. Schuler.

Things are different now,
With outlines and such,
We work twice as hard
But learn half as much.

(1945)

A Girl Named Alexander

Of all the names in history
From Moses down to Truman,
I've always had a favorite few,
Although I never knew them,
But in this hall of fame and flame
There's one that takes the cake,
And I call her Alexander,
Alexander, and she's great.

Little pug nose and pretty clothes,
A friendly disposition,
With sparkling eyes that can't disguise
The schemes you know she's wishing,
A teasing smile that drives you wild—
(A friendly means of persuasion),
A debonair flair for upswept hair
That comes down on certain occasions,
Tricky and vibrant, style with finesse,
And full of the dickens, more or less,
Alive and living and flirting with fate,
I call her Alexander—
Alexander, and she's great!

(1952)

Road Rage

As you roll forward, which one will you choose?
The rule of the road, or the role of the rude?
The rage of the road is the role of the rude,
Practiced by saints, and those who are crude;
Something goes wrong, and without premonition,
It all seems to start with engine ignition;
The docile acquire a very short fuse,
The rednecks get redder clear down to their shoes;
Everyone's ready, about to ignite,
Just waiting to start a roadrunner fight,
So are you a fighter, some kind of fool,
Or firm and controlled and rock solid cool?
Well, which will it be, which kind of dude,
The rule of the road, or the role of the rude?

(2000)

Ray E. Zarley
(1893–1961)

Ray E. Zarley, impatient man,
Ruled his kids with an iron hand;
Everyone knew in this family large,
There was no doubt, he was in charge.
Proud as a prince till his life was o'er,
But scarred from a life of being poor,
Worried most times over fact or rumor,
But tempered by a sense of humor
That carried him through the worst of times;
Along with his pride, he never resigned.
Farmer, inventor, carpenter too,
'Wasn't much he couldn't do;
Taught us a lot as the years went by,
Gave us a vision of what we should try,
Reader prolific, political sage,
Taught us all at an early age
Lessons from history, these we heard,
But FDR, an unpleasant word.
Loved his kids in a stern sort of way,
Worked us hard till the end of the day,
Loved our Mother, loved us all,
As our Father, Dad stood tall,
Wherever you are in the heavens above,
We still sense your pride,
Your pride and your love.
One-hundred years since he was born,
Lived a life of roses and thorns,
Ray E. Zarley, an important man,
Raised his kids with an even hand.

(1993)

Brennan

God came by just days ago;
The angels danced and sang,
As Brennan came to join us,
And the bells of Heaven rang.

A glimpse of her angelic face
Brings visions from above,
How one so small can generate
This tidal wave of love.

God bless this gentle child,
Surround her with your grace,
So her footprints on this planet
Will make a brighter place.

(2000)

Good Listener

An elephant's memory is very long,
They never forget the word of a song;
An unkind deed, or anything bad,
And everything good, and things that are sad,

No one knows how they seem to recall
Every event both great or small,
But the obvious reason, it appears
Is the very great size of both of their ears.

Yes, they listen big, they hear it all,
The thunder's clap, a leaf that falls,
So is there a lesson we can learn
From this marvelous beast who always discerns?

Well, just listen hard, and just get it all,
With ears that are big or ears that are small.

(2000)

Making Bread with Flour Green

A part of our family's Yuletide lore:
Awaiting a loaf from the Chefs next door.
A sumptuous treat with a taste of rye,
Better by far than eggnog pie.
But this year's bread—the best we've seen,
Made with care, and flour green.
Yes, flour green, a secret score,
Developed by the Chefs next door,
Advancing the art of making bread,
A new technique for years ahead.
The greatest advance we've ever seen,
Making bread with flour green.

(1997)

Christmas Greetings in Latin

Platotonium maximus letus adorium,
Comos almatum uno platorium,
Eureka excedo sub-zerorium
Forgeto, transmitto ad lettertorium.

HILARIUM BORNABUS

(translation)

On driving to work this morning, I remembered that tomorrow is your birthday. However, it is too cold to go get you a birthday card, so I'll send you a cheapie home-made one.

HAPPY BIRTHDAY!

Dixie Christmas

'Twas the night before Christmas and across the bay
The whitecaps were happy, Miami was gay;
The children weren't home yet—parties, instead,
With visions of grandeur and dancing ahead.

(While up to the north and out on the farm,
I was soaking my feet and just staying warm.)

When out on the sand there arose such a clatter,
They sprang to the beach to see what was the matter;
Away to the seashore they flew like a flash
And emptied their glasses and flicked off an ash.

And what to their wondering eyes should appear
But a white-bearded sailor in red underwear,
Crossing the water, tow rope and breeze;
They knew it was Santa by the snow on his skis.

(The moon on the breast of the new-fallen snow
Made me lonesome and cold—it was forty below.)

"As fallen leaves before the wild hurricanes fly,
And then like a scepter, mount to the sky,"
They all raised their glasses and drank down a toast
To this jolly old elf from the cold frozen coast.

It was half-past three when he found my place,
And I heard him exclaim as he de-iced his face,
"That Dixie run is a waste of time—,
You can't have Christmas in a Southern clime!"

"I give them a show year after year
But I can't wear my suit and I can't use my deer.
But this Southern trip, as a matter of fact,
Won't change my traditional Christmas act."

But I heard him exclaim as he drove out of sight,
"Merry Christmas, 'You-all,' and to all a good night."

(1955)

A Young Boy's Perception of a Wrigley Field Event

'Twas the climax of a ballgame,
The fans cheered long and high;
The sun was shining clear and bright
Into a cloudless sky.

The Cubs were whipping the Yankees,
Thanks to their pitching hero,
For by his speed and dazzling curves,
The score was three to zero.

All the bases were now loaded,
A result of three straight walks;
And up stepped the great Bambino
Into the batter's box.

He picked up his warclub
And tugged at his hat;
He stared at the pitcher
And across the plate he spat.

"Two are out in the last of the ninth,"
He recalled when the pitch had begun;
The sphere came down, it broke just right,
The umpire called, "Strike one!"

Bambino stepped up to the plate again,
It was up to him he knew;
The ball whizzed by, a perfect curve,
The umpire howled, "Strike two!"

Bambino calmly eyed the park,
His jaw was set and fixed;
He pointed to the right-field fence
As he waited for the pitch.

Down it came, hard and fast,
Babe gripped his bat much tighter;
He swung real hard and connected square
A ball never traveled lighter.

It cleared the fence ten feet or so,
The fans cheered long and loud;
The game was won by Babe's home run,
And it certainly thrilled the crowd.

Bambino tipped his hat and waved,
He'd done the best that he could;
A smile broke out on his face and he said,
"That time, I really made good."

(1943)

Why Do I Give?

There have been times in my life, and we've all been there,
When the world seemed hopeless, and I knelt in prayer,
And I pleaded with God to save the day, to light my path,
and show the way.

And then in ways I can't describe, the hand of God
    reversed the tide,
The waves and winds somehow stood still, and I sensed
    the touch of his Holy Will.

Why do I give? A debt I owe? Or gratitude, that leads me
    so?
All these and more, but most you see, I love my God, and
    He loves me.

(1985)

Marilyn

Whenever I'm gone on a trip far away,
When business is done, I never will stay;
Wherever I am, whenever I roam,
The first thing in mind is heading back home.

But home is a home if only you're there,
Without you a home would be empty and bare;
I never will change, so wherever I roam,
I'll rush back to you, to you and our home.

(1999)

The Midnight of Eternity

The light was burning dimly and could not erase the gloom,
As the twelve sat with the Master in the crowded upper room;
They could not sense His burden, or the danger, or the dread,
As the Master, speaking softly, served the wine and broke the bread
To symbolize His body and the shedding of His blood
For the ages to remember, and remember well they should.
The twelve were deeply troubled when they heard the Master say
That sitting at the table was he who would betray,
Then Peter, filled with passion, not understanding why,
Affirmed that for the Master he would suffer, he would die.

Jesus said, "I tell thee, Peter, that before the cock shall crow,
Ye shall thrice today deny me, that me ye even know."
And thence as He departed to a place, Gethsemane,
And anguish filled His utter soul, He fell upon his knees,
And prayed to God Almighty that the cup could pass, somehow,
"Thy Will, not mine, my Father," and the sweat rolled from His brow;
Alone He prayed intensely, so lonely, and He wept,
And His friends were keeping vigil, but He found that they had slept.
And while He spoke in these final hours to His friends on this infamous day,
Some torches approached as the plan began that would take the Master away.

From this group with their fiery brands stepped Judas, the twelfth of the band,
And crying, "Master, I know 'tis thee," he kissed Him on the hand,
And Judas' heart was frightened as he fled from the crowd,
With thirty pieces of silver hidden in his shroud,
The Master then was taken, and His hands were tightly bound,
And as the mob departed, His friends could not be found.
They took Him to Annas and there was arraigned
To plead His case, His Doctrine to explain,
"Why askest thou me, why seekest my word?
Go ask my accusers, for me they have heard."

And one of the soldiers then struck Him a blow,
"Answerest thou the High Priest so?"
And away He was taken to the palace ground
To the High Priest Caiaphas, still tightly bound;
And Peter who watched from the fringe of the crowd
Had twice been accused, but had stated aloud,
"This man is nothing, a stranger you see,
I never have known him, He's nothing to me,"
But as Peter was warmed by a fire close by,
A third accusation he chose to deny.

The Lord turned and looked toward the fire's faint glow,
As from the shadows the rooster did crow;
Peter then fled to a private place,
Remorse filled his soul as he wept in disgrace;
And Judas, too, repented himself, and to the chief priests cried,

"I have betrayed the innocent blood, His word I have
 defied."
"What is it to us?" the priests replied, "go and feed the
 poor,"
But thirty pieces of silver he cast on the temple floor;
And as the dawn began to break, scarcely could they see
The silhouette of Judas as he hanged there from a tree.

Away they led the Master, forsaken by His own,
Then away to Pilate, the governor from Rome,
Then asked Pilate earnestly, as if he were confused,
"Do you claim to be the King, the King of all the Jews?"
The mob was hushed as He raised His head;
Full and erect the Master replied, "Just as you have said!"
The crowd exploded, they accused Him more, this Man
 was truly hated;
Pilate marveled at the Prisoner's calm, for not a word He
 stated.
The Master was led to Herod's court, as Pilate chose to
 withdraw,
But Herod returned Him to Pilate again, for no wrong in
 the Master he saw.

Pilate implored the angry crowd, "There is no fault in this
 man!
I give his release at this Passover feast, as is custom here in
 your land."
Then cried the crowd, "Release not Him, give Barabbas
 relief,"
Now Barabbas was a robber, a robbing, murderous thief.
They platted a crown of thorns and forced it on His head,
And dressed Him in a purple robe; His handsome brow
 turned red;

They mocked and cursed the Master, and smote Him with their hands,
But Pilate amazed at His calmness, cried out, "Behold the Man!"
The mob was frenzied, as He was tied, they knew that He must die,
A thousand throats chorused the cry, and the word they shouted was "Crucify!"

They fashioned a cross from a tree long dead,
And the Master staggered from its weight as He led
That angry number with their passions full
Away to Golgotha, the place of the skull.
And the sky grew darker, and darker still
As the throng moved towards that lonely hill;
The nails in His hands, and then in His feet,
Not a cry pierced His lips as the task was complete;
And the cross was erect, not a light in the sky,
As the Lamb of God waited to die.

Pilate wrote a title, his conscience so bruised,
"Jesus of Nazareth, the King of the Jews."
But the priests did not want this sign o'er His head,
But Pilate in anger turned upon them and said,
"Take thou this Man whom thou hast smitten,
But I have written what I have written!"
Then as the ninth hour came, so dark they could not see,
He cried, "O God, my Father, hast Thou forsaken me?"
And then a moment later with His mother standing by,
On the midnight of eternity, the Lamb of God did die.

They gored His side; drew lots for His cloak, that the
    Scriptures might be fulfilled,
And the curtain was rent in the temple on the day that He
    was killed.
In an empty tomb they laid Him, not knowing of His call
That the grave would soon relinquish the Messiah of us
    all.
And so it was according to plan as created eons ago,
The Son of God should go to earth to die and suffer so;
Go to this place in the universe dwarfed by planets and
    stars,
Go to the rescue of all mankind, enslaved by sinful scars,
And so it was that the God of Ages delivered Himself to
    die,
That those who believe might claim his love and join Him
    one day in the sky.

(1966)

The Church Office and Indispensible Doris

Hey there, Doris, before you go,
Fix the coffee, and shovel the snow,
Look in on Bill, he's having a pout,
The light in the back has just burned out,
Read us our rights from the Golden Rule,
And fix the leak in the conference pool;
Please answer the phones just for today;
Write me a speech so I'll know what to say,
Then dust our books and pay our dues,
And lick the stamps for *Christian News*.

There's another list, an item or two,
Of things that no one else can do;
Phone the mayor and call his bluff,
His last check just wasn't enough;
Call the V.P. and give him the sack,
And get the old man off my back;
The old stock market's not doing well,
So should we buy, or should we sell?
And make a list (there are a few)
Of other important things to do,
And when you're done, it will be night,
So lock the doors, turn off the lights.

We never thought that you would go,
But now we know that it is so,
Hey, Dear Doris, we know it's true,
There's not a thing that you can't do;
You've done it all, and done it well,
But now we ring the farewell bell;
And after you're gone for only a day,
Our very first note will arrive and say,

"Hey there, Doris, how have you been?
And when are you coming home again?
Hey there, Doris, don't stay long,
We miss your love, we miss your song."
And as time goes by, and you're hard to find,
The same dear question will come to mind:
"Hey there, Doris, how have you been?
And when are you coming home again?"

(1997)

Poet's Lament

I can't sing and I can't paint,
No use being what I ain't,
But I write poems pretty good,
Tho' some still question if I should.

I can't speak and I can't dance,
Do things by the seat of my pants,
But I write verses fast and free;
No one reads them much but me.

But, after all is said and done,
And life is o'er, the races run,
May someone say, he wasn't much,
Except for verse, he had a touch.

(1990)